Multilevel Modeling for Social and Personality Psychology

The SAGE Library of Methods in Social and Personality Psychology is a new series of books to provide students and researchers in these fields with an understanding of the methods and techniques essential to conducting cutting-edge research.

Each volume explains a specific topic and has been written by an active scholar (or scholars) with expertise in that particular methodological domain. Assuming no prior knowledge of the topic, the volumes are clear and accessible for all readers. In each volume, a topic is introduced, applications are discussed, and readers are led step by step through worked examples. In addition, advice about how to interpret and prepare results for publication is presented.

The Library should be particularly valuable for advanced students and academics who want to know more about how to use research methods and who want experience-based advice from leading scholars in social and personality psychology.

Published titles:
Jim Blascovich, Eric J. Vanman, Wendy Berry Mendes, Sally Dickerson, *Social Psychophysiology for Social and Personality Psychology*

R. Michael Furr, *Scale Construction and Psychometrics for Social and Personality Psychology*

Rick H. Hoyle, *Structural Equation Modeling for Social and Personality Psychology*

John B. Nezlek, *Multilevel Modeling for Social and Personality Psychology*

Laurie A. Rudman, *Implicit Measures for Social and Personality Psychology*

Forthcoming titles:
John B. Nezlek, *Diary Methods for Social and Personality Psychology*

The SAGE Library of Methods in Social and Personality Psychology

Multilevel Modeling for Social and Personality Psychology

John B. Nezlek

Los Angeles | London | New Delhi
Singapore | Washington DC

First published 2011

SAGE Publications Ltd
1 Oliver's Yard
55 City Road
London ECIY ISP

SAGE Publications Inc.
2455 Teller Road
Thousand Oaks, California 91320

SAGE Publications India Pvt Ltd
B 1/I 1 Mohan Cooperative Industrial Area
Mathura Road
New Delhi 110 044

SAGE Publications Asia-Pacific Pte Ltd
33 Pekin Street #20-01
Far East Square
Singapore 048763

Library of Congress Control Number: 2010935085

British Library Cataloguing in Publication data

A catalogue record for this book is available from the British Library

ISBN 978-0-85702-401-5

Typeset by C&M Digitals (P) Ltd, Chennai, India
Printed by MPG Books Group, Bodmin, Cornwall
Printed on paper from sustainable resources

Contents

1 Introduction   1

2 Multilevel Random Coefficient Models: Basics   9

3 Multilevel Random Coefficient Models: Some Advanced Topics   35

4 Conceptualizing the Multilevel Structure   53

5 Using HLM   71

References   105

Resources   107

Index   109

1

Introduction

"Once you know that hierarchies exist, you see them everywhere." I have used this quote by Kreft and de Leeuw (1998) frequently when writing about why, when, and how to use multilevel models and when giving workshops on multilevel modeling. I start this way because I think learning about multilevel modeling meaningfully changes how people think about their research. It can change how they think about data they have already collected (the data are multilevel and this was not recognized or was not taken into account), it can change how they think about the data they will collect, and it can change how they think about the questions they will ask and answer.

It is always frustrating to me when I have a question and perhaps a sense of what type of information (raw data) might be used to answer that question, but I have no idea how I would analyze such data if I collected them. How would I compile the statistics that would answer my question? What statistics would be best? Moreover, I assume that others share this frustration (actually, I know this). For those of you who are not familiar with multilevel modeling, the overarching goal of this volume is to change how you think about your data and the questions they can answer: to expand the tools you have at your disposal so that you can think about different (perhaps better) questions with the knowledge of how you can answer these new questions. Even for those of you who are somewhat familiar with multilevel modeling, some of the techniques I discuss may expand your repertoire.

Certainly, much of this volume will be about the "nuts and bolts" of multilevel modeling. How does one build a multilevel model? How does one test different hypotheses and interpret the results? How on earth do you write this stuff up? And so forth. Nevertheless, the overarching goal is conceptual. The nuts and bolts are just that, simple tools, means to ends. The real prize is the ability to understand phenomena more clearly, to separate relationships that exist at different levels of analysis, and to avoid confounding relationships across levels of analysis.

In service of this conceptual goal, my primary and immediate goal in writing this volume is to help you understand what multilevel modeling is, why it is useful for social and personality psychologists, and how to conduct, interpret, and describe multilevel analyses. The volume is intended for people who know nothing or very little about multilevel analyses and who want to learn how to conduct multilevel analyses, and for people who simply want to read an article that uses multilevel modeling and have some idea of what was done. It is not technically focused; rather, it provides a rationale for multilevel modeling, describes critical features of the technique, and discusses different applications. Throughout, examples are provided that are particularly relevant to social and personality psychologists.

Those of you who are already familiar with multilevel modeling may find that after reading this volume you work more efficiently and with more confidence. In the case of some of the sections that focus on specific aspects of the technique, you may find that they enhance and sharpen your skills. By the way, in terms of statistical background and experience, you will need to be somewhat familiar with regression analysis – simple OLS (ordinary least squares) regression. To take full advantage of some of the "tricks" that I describe, it will be beneficial but not necessary for you to be familiar with different ways of coding grouping variables, dummy codes, contrast codes, etc.

The style of this volume is not the same as that of many contemporary articles in social and personality psychology; each statement I make will not be supported by a slew of references. Points that are not controversial (at least in my mind) will simply be stated as fact. When there is some uncertainty, this will be mentioned. There will be references here and there so that those of you who are starved for citations will find sustenance, however meager it may be. My decision to write this way was motivated by my desire to inform and to instruct while not debating the merits of distinctions that are meaningful only to those who are well informed, however important and necessary such distinctions and debates may be.

Moreover, there will be times when I make recommendations based solely upon my experience: what has happened to my data, what I have found that works or does not work, etc. There are a lot of aspects of multilevel modeling that are not well understood, and I am certain that I have missed some recent developments. I am not a statistician *per se*. I am an experienced and (in my own humble opinion) a well-informed user. Regardless, I can assure you that in all the cases I discuss, I have analyzed numerous data sets in different ways, with different options, simply to see what matters and how it matters. I hope that this volume encourages you to do the same. Any statistical procedure is a tool, and understanding what it does can be thought of as a science, but applying it judiciously is an art. So, read this volume and learn how to mix colors so that you will be able to paint your own masterpiece.

Most of the examples I will use will be from my own published research. I do this not because I think my research is better than anyone else's. Rather, I use examples from my own work because I am more familiar with the subtleties of the data and the analyses, and I could use and re-analyze my own data more easily than the data collected by other scholars. Off we go. By the way, I will often use the abbreviation MLM for multilevel modeling.

What is meant by the term "multilevel"?

The term "multilevel" refers to the fact that observations, sometimes called units of analysis, are collected (or sampled) at multiple levels of analysis simultaneously. Okay, that's a bit circular. It may help to note that multilevel data sets are sometimes referred to as "nested" or "hierarchically nested" because observations at one level of analysis are nested within observations at another level. Statisticians also use the phrase "clustered" and sometimes talk about observations being clustered within a common cluster. I will use the term "nested" because its use is more widespread than "clustered."

If for a study of academic achievement data were collected in 20 classrooms with 10–20 students in each classroom, this would create a multilevel data set, with students nested or clustered within classes. In such a study, data are collected describing units of analysis at different levels of analysis. At the classroom level, class size or years of teacher's experience might be measured. Such measures exist only as classroom characteristics that are shared by all students in a specific classroom. In contrast, at the student level, grades and amount of study, measures that might vary among the students within a single classroom, might also be collected.

Similarly, multiple observations about a single person might be collected in some type of diary study. In such a study, daily observations (e.g., daily observations of mood) would be treated as nested within persons. Person level measures such as gender or some type of personality trait would exist at the person level, and the daily level observations for each person would have these characteristics in common. In contrast, at the daily level, data describing the events that occurred each day and how an individual thought about him or herself that day might be collected. Later, I describe how to conceptualize levels of analysis.

An important aspect of multilevel sampling is that analyses of multilevel data need to take into account the error associated with sampling at multiple levels of analysis. Social and personality psychologists are accustomed to thinking of the sampling error associated with sampling individuals. Nevertheless, in the typical multilevel study a sample of some unit of analysis other than people has been drawn. In a diary study in which the focus of attention is on within-person relationships between daily measures (e.g., relationships between stressful daily events and daily affect), there is some error associated with the sampling of the days over which the study took place. Coefficients describing such relationships that are based on a particular two weeks in a person's life when the study was conducted will typically be similar to, but not the same as, coefficients based on a different two-week period. That is, the coefficients themselves have a sampling error different from, and above and beyond, the sampling error associated with sampling persons. Similarly, when individuals are nested within groups, there are two targets of inference – individuals and groups. The groups in such studies are meant to be representative of the population of groups.

The "multi" in "multilevel" also refers to the fact that relationships and the phenomena they are meant to represent can exist and be examined simultaneously at different levels of analysis (or different levels of aggregation). In the above classroom example, one could examine relationships between amount of study and grades at the between-class level (Are average grades higher in classes in which students study more on average?) or at the within-class or student level (Do students who study more have higher grades?). More subtly, one could determine if individual level relationships between grades and studying varied across classrooms. As discussed below, relationships at these two levels of analysis are mathematically and statistically independent. It is theoretically possible to have positive relationships at one level of analysis and negative relationships at another. Technically, knowing the classroom level relationship between studying and grades tells us nothing about the student level relationship between these same two measures.

Traditionally, the levels of a multilevel model are referred to by number – level 1, level 2, and so forth – with larger numbers indicating levels higher in the hierarchy. So, in the previous example, data describing individual students would be level 1 data (could also be called student level), and data describing classrooms would be level 2 data (could also be called classroom level). In this volume, I will focus on two-level models because they illustrate the principle well and because two levels will be sufficient for most applications. Although the number of levels is theoretically limitless, as discussed below, there are reasons to follow the advice offered by the adage "Less is more."

To me, one of the most powerful advantages obtained by understanding MLM is the fact that the same principles (and techniques) can be applied to data describing vastly different phenomena. Just as we can think of students nested within classrooms, it is only a small step to think of workers nested within work groups or patients/clients nested within therapists, clinics, or treatment centers. Although perhaps not as obvious, as suggested above, it is just another small step to think of diary data in which observations (e.g., daily reports) are nested within persons.

The same modeling techniques hold whether people are nested within groups or observations are nested within persons. Admittedly, there are some concerns that are more important for one broad type of data than for others. For example, autocorrelated errors (the possibility that errors of measurement for observations collected over time are correlated) might be a concern when analyzing some types of diary data, whereas they would not be a concern for a study in which people were nested within groups. Nevertheless, there are more similarities among the MLM procedures appropriate for substantively different data structures than there are differences among such procedures. In learning terms, there is considerable positive transfer of understanding the techniques needed to analyze the data in one substantive domain to another.

NB: most multilevel modelers use the term "group" to refer to an organizing unit, even when an organizing unit is not an actual group. For example, in a diary study in which days are nested within persons, within the lexicon of MLM, people are referred to as groups. Admittedly, referring to individuals as groups can be confusing, but within MLM the use of the term "group" in this way is so deeply ingrained that it is unavoidable at present. Perhaps with time the term "cluster" will replace "group," but for now we will have to grin and bear it.

Varying relationships across different levels of analysis

The importance of taking into account the nested or multilevel structure of a data set reflects (in part) the possibility, perhaps the likelihood, that relationships between constructs at different levels of analysis vary. For example, assume we have collected data describing how much students, who are nested within classrooms, study, and we also know their grades. One way to analyze such data would be to calculate for each classroom the average amount students study each week and the average grade they receive, and correlate these two measures. This is sometimes referred to as an analysis of aggregates. Such a correlation would answer the question, "Are grades higher in classes in which students study more compared to classes in which students study less?"

This is an appropriate question, but it is not the same question as, "Do students who study more get higher grades?" This second question refers to a relationship at the level of the individual student, not at the level of the classroom. As illustrated by the data in Table 1, it is entirely possible to have one type of relationship (positive v. negative) at one level of analysis and another relationship at the other level of analysis. In the first panel, the relationship between grades and studying within each class is negative, whereas the relationship at the between-class level (between-class averages) is positive. In contrast, in the second panel, the relationship between grades and studying within each class is positive, whereas the relationship at the between-class level is negative. In the third panel, the within-class relationships vary. Relationships at the two levels of analysis are mathematically independent. Knowing the relationship at one level of analysis tells us nothing (technically speaking) about relationships at the other level of analysis.

In case you are having trouble thinking about how a correlation between studying and grades at the between-class level does not accurately represent relationships at the student level, consider the following example. In the clinical literature, anxiety and depression are "comorbid." People who are anxious tend to be depressed and vice-versa. Moreover, such a relationship is assumed by most

Table 1   Varying relationships across levels of analyses

Panel 1 Negative within-class relationship, positive between-class relationship

	Class 1		Class 2		Class 3	
	Grades	*Study*	*Grades*	*Study*	*Grades*	*Study*
	2.1	6	3.1	8	3.3	10
	2.2	5	3.2	7	3.4	9
	2.3	4	3.3	6	3.5	8
	2.4	3	3.4	5	3.6	7
	2.5	2	3.5	4	3.7	6
Mean	2.3	4	3.3	6	3.5	8

Panel 2 Positive within-class relationship, negative between-class relationship

	Class 1		Class 2		Class 3	
	Grades	*Study*	*Grades*	*Study*	*Grades*	*Study*
	2.1	6	3.1	4	3.3	2
	2.2	7	3.2	5	3.4	3
	2.3	8	3.3	6	3.5	4
	2.4	9	3.4	7	3.6	5
	2.5	10	3.5	8	3.7	6
Mean	2.3	8	3.3	6	3.5	4

Panel 3 Variable within-class relationship, positive between-class relationship

	Class 1		Class 2		Class 3	
	Grades	*Study*	*Grades*	*Study*	*Grades*	*Study*
	2.1	2	3.1	8	3.3	10
	2.2	3	3.2	5	3.4	9
	2.3	4	3.3	6	3.5	8
	2.4	5	3.4	7	3.6	7
	2.5	6	3.5	4	3.7	6
Mean	2.3	4	3.3	6	3.5	8

measures of the Big Five factor of neuroticism. Most measures of neuroticism have items such as "depressed, blue" and "gets nervous easily." Nevertheless, at any moment in time, it may be difficult for people to be both depressed and anxious because depression is a type of deactive affect, whereas anxiety is a type of active affect. At the within-person (moment to moment) level, depression and anxiety may be negatively related or unrelated, whereas at the between-person level (how depressed and anxious a person is, in general, on average), the two may be positively related. See Cervone (2004) and Affleck, Zautra, Tennen, and Armeli (1999) for discussions of the value of distinguishing between- and within-person levels of analysis when considering individual differences.

Returning to our classroom example, as indicated by the data in Table 1, within-group relationships (for our example, the individual or within-classroom level) can vary, and one of the advantages of the techniques discussed in this volume is the ability to model such variability. Why is the relationship between grades and studying stronger in some classes than in others? Similarly, at the within-person level, relationships between measures can vary. Why is the within-person relationship between daily stressors and anxiety stronger for some people than for others? One of the important advantages of multilevel analyses over single level analyses is that they allow for the possibility that relationships between measures vary across units of analysis (groups at level 2). Moreover, MLM provides statistically accurate and efficient estimates of how between-unit (level 2) differences can account for within-unit (level 1) differences in relationships.

When relationships vary across levels of analysis or across units within the same level of analysis, such situations beg questions about which is the "correct" relationship. What's the right answer? Unfortunately, there is no simple answer to such questions. The correct answer depends upon the question. If the question concerns between-group relationships, then analyses at the between-group level provide the answer. If the question concerns within-group relationships, then analyses that describe within-group relationships provide the answer, with the caveat that within-group relationships may vary.

Different ways of analyzing multilevel data

Over time, nested data have been analyzed in various ways other than using the techniques I discuss here (what are technically referred to as multilevel random coefficient models – see next chapter), and in this section I critically review these approaches. Most of these previous methods rely on some type of OLS analysis, and although with the increasing popularity of multilevel modeling these types of analyses are appearing less and less often, as Santayana warned, "Those who cannot remember the past are condemned to repeat it," and so it will be instructive to review briefly such approaches.

Broadly speaking, in the past, multilevel data have sometimes been analyzed with what have been called "aggregation" and "disaggregation" techniques. In aggregation analyses, group means are calculated and relationships are examined at the between-group level. Although aggregation analyses can be appropriate (depending upon the level at which a question is posed), researchers who rely on them are prone to commit what is commonly referred to as the ecological fallacy (Robinson, 1950). Researchers commit the ecological fallacy when they use relationships at the between-group level to draw conclusions about relationships at the within-group level. Robinson's classic paper was based on analyses of the 1930 US Census. Using aggregates calculated within each state, he found a positive between-state relationship between literacy rates and the percentage of residents that were immigrants. States that had more immigrants had higher literacy rates. In contrast, he found negative relationships within states, i.e., the literacy rate among immigrants was lower than it was among those who were native born. Such possibilities are also illustrated by the data presented in Table 1, particularly the data in the first two panels.

In disaggregation analyses, analyses are conducted at level 1 (in a two-level data set). In such analyses, level 2 measures are "brought down" to level 1 (level 2 measures are repeated for all the level 1 units nested within their corresponding level 2 unit) and treated as if they were level 1 measures. In a diary study, this would entail assigning individual differences such as personality measures with each day of data a person provided. In a group study, it would entail assigning group level measures to all of the individuals in a group.

An important characteristic of nested data is that level 1 observations are not fully independent. The members of a group have the characteristics of their group in common, and the social interactions a person describes have the characteristics of the person describing them in common. Such a lack of independence means that techniques such as OLS regression in which level 1 observations are the sole units of analysis cannot be used because such analyses violate a fundamental assumption of such analyses – the independence of observations. In a study of groups, it is incorrect to append group level data to each of the individuals in a group and then conduct a single level analysis with the individuals as the unit of analysis. Likewise, in a diary study, it is incorrect to append individual (person level) data such as personality characteristics to the daily diary data and then conduct single level analyses with the day as the unit of analysis.

Such analyses have other important shortcomings. Of particular importance is that they assume that the level 1 (within-unit) relationships are consistent across level 2 units. This is even the case if a least-squared dummy variable analysis is used (LSDV: e.g., Cohen & Cohen, 1983). In LSDV analyses, the group member-ship of the level 1 units is represented by a series of $k - 1$ dummy-coded (0, 1) variables, where k is the number of groups. LSDV analyses do take into account the possibility (actually, the likelihood) that the means of level 1 predictors vary across level 2 units, but they do not take into account the possibility (again, the likelihood) that relationships between these level 1 variables vary across level 2 units. Such a possibility can be addressed by including terms representing the interaction between the group variables (the dummy codes) and the various pre-dictors. Nonetheless, aside from practical considerations (e.g., 100 level 2 units and two predictors would require just under 200 level 1 predictors), as discussed above, such analyses do not model error properly. In a multilevel study there are two sampling distributions, and because LSDV analyses are OLS, they can have only one error term. See Nezlek (2001) for a discussion of the shortcomings of various types of OLS analyses of multilevel data.

2

Multilevel Random Coefficient Models: Basics

Logic of multilevel analyses

In describing the logic of multilevel modeling, I follow the logic offered by Bryk and Raudenbush (1992) in their pioneering book. I use the term "pioneering" because they were the first (to my knowledge) to describe multilevel models as a series of equations in which coefficients from one level of analysis are "passed up" to the next level of analysis. Conceptually, I think this makes more sense than thinking of a multilevel model as a single equation with a sometimes horrifying number of terms. Nevertheless, for different reasons, at times it is helpful to remember that underlying the "separate equations model" I use for pedagogical purposes is a single equation with potentially lots of unknowns to estimate.

In terms of a study of academic achievement, a simple example of this "passing up" is an analysis examining the relationship between the average grade students in each class receive and the years of experience their teachers have. Conceptually, this is similar to calculating an average grade for each class and then correlating this average grade with the experience of the teachers of these classes. A slightly more complex example would be examining the individual (student level) relationship between grades and studying. A correlation could be calculated for each class and then some type of average correlation could be estimated. Moreover, such a correlation could then in turn be correlated with teacher experience. For example, is the relationship between grades and studying weaker for more experienced teachers, perhaps because they are more effective in the classroom? In both these cases, the correlation between grades and studying is "passed up" from the student level to the classroom level. In the first instance, the correlations are passed up solely to obtain an average, whereas in the second, they are passed up to model differences among them.

Similarly, in a diary style study, one might calculate a mean representing the average anxiety a person experiences each day and correlate that with a between-person measure such as self-esteem. Or, one might calculate within-person correlations representing the relationship between anxiety and daily stress and pass this correlation up to the person level, either to estimate some type of average or typical relationship or to analyze individual differences in such relationships.

For example, is the relationship between stress and anxiety stronger for people higher in neuroticism than it is for people lower in neuroticism?

So, what's wrong with calculating such averages or correlations and doing such analyses? Simply put, the estimates they provide of relationships such as those I just discussed are not as accurate as the estimates provided by multilevel random coefficient analyses – the type of analyses described in this volume. For example, the reliability of a mean (the extent to which a mean represents the responses of a group) varies as a function of the sample size and the within-group variance. Consider the following two sets of six observations: 1, 1, 1, 9, 9, 9, and 4, 4, 5, 5, 6, 6. Although the mean for both sets of data is 5.0, the second 5 is a "better" 5 than the first because the scores in the second group cluster more closely around 5 than the scores in the first group. Analyses based upon aggregates such as those described above that do not take into account the consistency of the responses in the groups that are used as the basis for the aggregation (in more formal terms, the reliability of the mean) will not estimate relationships as accurately as analyses that take such differences into account, and MLM does this. The same situation exists with correlations, although the difference between the results of MLM and OLS analyses of within-group correlations is greater than it is for analyses of means. This is due in part to the fact that the reliability of a correlation is a function of the sample size, the size of the correlation, and the reliability of the measures that are being correlated.

Basic models/equations

The logic of multilevel modeling can also be illustrated through the use of the equations that underlie different models, and throughout this volume, I will describe multilevel models using such equations. It can clarify what has been done, and given the complexities of the analyses, I think this is needed. Moreover, I will use the explanatory framework offered by Bryk and Raudenbush (1992) in which they present the equations for each level of an analysis separately. To me, this makes absolutely clear what is predicting what. The nomenclature is simple, and relationships within and across levels are easy to distinguish.

Regardless, keep in mind that in reality, all coefficients at all levels of analysis are estimated simultaneously. This means that the underlying model can also be represented by a single equation in which an outcome is being modeled as a function of the intercepts at each level of analysis, the predictors at each level, and the error terms. I find such equations sort of mind-numbing, so I go with the Bryk and Raudenbush approach. Nonetheless, there are times when the single equation representation is informative, and it has been my experience that understanding the single equation representation is easier after you understand the "separate equation" representation I use here.

I will introduce and discuss modeling in terms of two-level models of continuous outcomes. Later, I describe some three-level models, which involve simple extensions of the logic underlying two-level models – or at least it should be simple by then. The techniques that are needed for non-linear outcomes are slightly different (technically) from the techniques for continuous outcomes, although the logic of the analyses is similar. I discuss non-linear outcomes in a separate section in Chapter 3. Note that detailed descriptions of analyses similar to those discussed in these initial sections are presented in Chapter 5, "Using HLM."

So, let's start with a two-level model in which persons are nested within groups. In what is close to the standard nomenclature, level 1 coefficients are represented with βs, with coefficients for intercepts subscripted 0, those for the first coefficient subscripted 1, those for the second coefficient subscripted 2, and so forth. The equation for the basic level 1 model is:

$$y_{ij} = \beta_{0j} + r_{ij}$$

In such a model, for outcome y, there are i level 1 observations that are treated as nested within j level 2 groups. The level 1 observations are modeled simply as a function of the mean for each group (the intercept β_{0j}) and the deviation of each observation in a group from the mean of that group (r_{ij}). The variance of r_{ij} is the within-group level 1 variance. The total within-group variance is the sum of the within-group variances for each of the j groups in the data. In essence, this level 1 variability is an indication of how well the group means represent the scores in the groups: that is, how much do the observations in a group vary from their group means?

Level 1 coefficients are then modeled at level 2, and there is a separate level 2 equation for each level 1 coefficient. Level 2 coefficients are represented with γs. The basic level 2 model is:

$$\beta_{0j} = \gamma_{00} + \mu_{0j}$$

In this equation, the intercept of y for each of the j level 2 units of analysis (β_{0j}) is modeled as a function of the mean of intercepts (γ_{00} – in this case, the mean of means) and the deviation of the intercept from each group from this mean (μ_{0j}). The variance of μ_{0j} is the level 2 variance: that is, how much do the intercepts for each group (in this case, the means for each group) vary? In terms of the nomenclature, the first subscript for a level 2 coefficient represents the level 1 coefficient being modeled, and the second subscript represents the level 2 coefficient. So, we know that γ_{00} represents something about the intercept being brought up from level 1 (because the first subscript is 0), and more specifically, we know that it is the intercept of this coefficient because the second subscript is 0.

When these two basic models are combined, this is referred to as a totally unconditional (or null) model because there are no predictors at any level of analysis. Unconditional models are valuable because they provide an estimate of how the total variability of a set of measures can be divided among the levels of an analysis.

11

Predictors can be added to this basic model at either level of analysis. Assume a study in which students are nested within classes, and the outcome measure is a test score. At the within-class (individual) level, the relationship between test scores and ability (as measured by a standard test) could be examined with the following model:

$$y_{ij} = \beta_{0j} + \beta_{1j} \,(\text{Ability}) + r_{ij}$$
$$\beta_{0j} = \gamma_{00} + \mu_{0j}$$
$$\beta_{1j} = \gamma_{10} + \mu_{1j}$$

In this model, the intercept of y (β_{0j}) for each of j level 2 classes is modeled as a function of the mean intercept (γ_{00}) and error (μ_{0j}), and the slope (β_{1j}) representing the within-class relationship between scores and ability for each of j classes is modeled as a function of the mean slope ($\gamma_{10,}$ the average slope, i.e., the relationship between score and ability, across all classes) and error (μ_{1j}).

In MLM, coefficients are tested for significance against 0, and in this model, the significance test of the mean slope (is the mean slope significantly different from 0?) is made at level 2, via the γ_{10} coefficient. If the γ_{10} coefficient is significantly different from 0, then the null hypothesis is rejected. The intercept is also tested for significance via the γ_{00} coefficient: is the mean intercept significantly different from 0? The meaning of these tests, i.e., what the coefficients represent, will vary as a function of the measures themselves, and most importantly, the meaning will vary as a function of how the level 1 predictors are centered, a topic discussed in the next section.

In MLM, the random error terms for level 1 coefficients (the μ_{0j} and μ_{1j} terms) are also tested for significance, and such significance tests can be used to make decisions about including or excluding random error terms from models. When an error term for a coefficient is included in a model, the coefficient is referred to as a random coefficient, and when an error term is not included, the coefficient is referred to as a fixed coefficient. Various characteristics of random error terms are discussed in the section "Modeling Error" later in this chapter.

Predictors can also be added at level 2. Continuing the above example, at the between-class level, the relationship between test scores and teacher's emotional intelligence (EI) could be examined with the following model:

$$y_{ij} = \beta_{0j} + r_{ij}$$
$$\beta_{0j} = \gamma_{00} + \gamma_{01} \,(\text{EI}) + \mu_{0j}$$

In this model, the mean score for a class (the β_{0j} brought up from level 1) is being modeled as a function of the grand mean and the EI of a teacher. If the γ_{01} coefficient is significantly different from 0, then there is a relationship between a teacher's EI and the average score for students in his or her class. Once again, precisely what these level 2 coefficients represent will vary as a function of how the level 2 predictors are centered.

Predictors can be added at both levels of analysis simultaneously. Relationships between test scores and ability of study could be examined at the individual level, and in turn, classroom level differences in these relationships could be modeled at the between-class level as a function of teacher EI. Analyses examining such relationships are sometimes called "slopes as outcomes" analyses because a slope (a relationship) from a lower level (e.g., level 1) becomes an outcome at an upper level (e.g., level 2).

$$y_{ij} = \beta_{0j} + \beta_{1j} \text{ (Ability)} + r_{ij}$$
$$\beta_{0j} = \gamma_{00} + \gamma_{01} \text{ (EI)} + \mu_{0j}$$
$$\beta_{1j} = \gamma_{10} + \gamma_{11} \text{ (EI)} + \mu_{1j}$$

In this model, the slope for each class (β_{1j}) is brought up from level 1 and is modeled as a function of the mean and the EI of a teacher. If the γ_{11} coefficient is significantly different from 0, then the relationship between test scores and ability varies as a function of teacher EI. Note that EI is included in both level 2 equations, a topic discussed below.

In the most recent version of the HLM program (6.0), which I discuss below, different nomenclatures are used for models in which persons are nested within groups and observations are nested within persons. The traditional βs and γs are used when people are nested within groups, but these have been changed to πs and βs when observations are nested within people. (In these two systems, people are always represented by βs.) The models and the results of analyses do not vary as a function of which sets of letters are used. The distinction is purely terminological.

Similar to OLS regression, these multilevel models are simply templates that can be applied to various types of data structures. In a study of therapeutic outcomes, clients could be nested within therapists or clinics. In diary style studies, observations (days or certain types of events such as social interactions) could be nested within persons. In studies relying upon reaction times, responses can be treated as nested within persons and experimental conditions can be modeled at the person level. Such applications are limited only by the insight of researchers and their ability to collect the necessary data.

Centering

How predictors are centered is one of the critical aspects of MLM analyses. In the lexicon of MLM, "centering" refers to the reference value from which deviations are taken. For analysts steeped in the OLS tradition, centering can be difficult to comprehend for two reasons. First, MLM analyses produce only unstandardized coefficients, and in such analyses, the intercept is meaningful, particularly the level 1 intercept. In contrast, in most OLS analyses, the intercept is typically ignored; analysts look at the standardized coefficients, and that's that. As discussed later, controlling the intercept is critical to fine tuning MLM analyses, and the effects of different centering options will also be illustrated using analyses of the sample data set: see Chapter 5, "Using HLM." Also, for those looking for a more technically focused explanation, I recommend Enders and Tofighi (2007).

Second, in OLS regression analysis, relationships are based on deviations from the mean. In the simplest terms, a correlation is an indication of how closely the deviations of observations from the mean of one variable correspond to the deviations of another variable. A correlation of 1 means that the deviations of observations on measure X correspond perfectly to the deviations from the mean on a measure Y. A correlation of 0 means that there is absolutely no correspondence between the deviations from the mean of X and the deviations from the mean of Y.

In MLM, there are various ways to define the reference point around which deviations are taken, and these are referred to as centering options. For those familiar with OLS analyses, the easiest set of options to consider are those at level 2 (or level 3 in a three-level model). At these levels, there are two options, grand-mean centered and zero centered (sometimes referred to as uncentered; in keeping with the use in the literature, I will use uncentered and zero centered interchangeably – get used to it).

Grand-mean centering is the same type of centering that is used in OLS regression, and when predictors are grand-mean centered, the intercept represents the expected value for an observation that is at the grand mean of a predictor, i.e., when the deviation between a predictor and the mean of the predictor is 0. At level 2, when predictors are grand-mean centered, the coefficients are the functional equivalents of those generated in OLS regression. In contrast, when predictors are uncentered, deviations are calculated from 0, and the intercept represents the expected value for an observation that has a value of 0 on a predictor.

Let's extend the previous example on test scores. Assume the following model. The level 1 model is unconditional, which means that the level 1 intercept (β_{0j}) represents the mean score for each class.

$$y_{ij} = \beta_{0j} + r_{ij}$$
$$\beta_{0j} = \gamma_{00} + \gamma_{01} (EI) + \mu_{0j}$$

If EI (teacher's emotional intelligence) is entered grand-mean centered, then the intercept of the intercepts (γ_{00}) represents the expected value for a level 2 observation for which the value of the predictor is at the mean. In this case, this is the expected value for the intercept from level 1 (β_{0j}, the class average) for a class that has a teacher with a mean EI score.

What if EI is entered zero centered? Then the intercept of the intercepts (γ_{00}) represents the expected value for a level 2 observation (a class) for which EI = 0. Well, what if 0 is not a valid value for EI? Well, then don't enter it uncentered. By the way, even if 0 is not a valid value the program will run the analysis (it does not know any better), but it will estimate a model that is not particularly meaningful, i.e., it will estimate an intercept that has no meaning.

Zero centering can make sense, however, when 0 is a valid value for a predictor. Assume that Sex is a level 2 predictor, coded 1 = women, 0 = men.

$$y_{ij} = \beta_{0j} + r_{ij}$$
$$\beta_{0j} = \gamma_{00} + \gamma_{01} (Sex) + \mu_{0j}$$

If Sex is entered uncentered, then γ_{00} represents the expected value for γ_{00} when Sex = 0, which in this case means the expected value for a class with a male teacher. The easiest way to understand this is to do a quick substitution. For male teachers, Sex = 0, and so whatever the effect is for Sex drops out when Sex is set to 0. More about this later in this chapter in the section "Categorical predictors and examining differences among groups." If you enter Sex grand-mean centered, then the intercept will represent the mean intercept adjusted for the distribution of the sex of teachers.

At level 1 in a two-level model (and at levels 1 and 2 in a three-level model), there are three centering options: grand-mean, zero, and group-mean. Although how predictors are centered is not trivial at level 2, centering tends to be more important at level 1 than it is at level 2 because centering changes the meaning of the intercept, and the level 1 intercept is being "brought up" to level 2. That is, by changing how predictors are centered at level 1 you change what is being analyzed at level 2. I expand on this below and in the section on categorical predictors.

Now, let's extend the previous example by including a predictor, ability at level 1. To keep the discussion simple, there are no predictors at level 2. The level 1 model looks like this.

$$y_{ij} = \beta_{0j} + \beta_{1j} (Ability) + r_{ij}$$
$$\beta_{0j} = \gamma_{00} + \mu_{0j}$$
$$\beta_{1j} = \gamma_{10} + \mu_{1j}$$

When level 1 predictors are entered uncentered, the intercept for each group represents the expected value for an observation when a predictor equals 0. In many ways, this is the same as it was for level 2 predictors, except in this case, it is the intercept for each group that is being estimated (β_{0j}), and it is a level 1 predictor that is being considered. In our example, if Ability was entered uncentered, then the intercept would represent the expected score in each classroom for a student who had no ability (Ability = 0). As before, what happens if a level 1 predictor for which 0 is not a valid value (e.g., a 1–7 scale) is entered uncentered? Nothing much, other than you are estimating a parameter under conditions that cannot exist, which is not the best practice.

When level 1 predictors are entered grand-mean centered, the intercept for each group represents the expected value for an observation for which the level 1 predictor is at the grand mean for the predictor. This is similar to what grand-mean centering was for level 2 predictors, except in this case, it is the intercept for each group that is being estimated (β_{0j}) and it is a level 1 predictor that is being considered. In our example, if Ability was entered grand-mean centered, then the intercept would represent the expected score in each classroom for a student who had average ability, with "average" in this case being defined in terms of all the students in the study.

Finally, when level 1 predictors are entered group-mean centered, the intercept for each group represents the expected value for an observation for which the level 1 predictor is at the group mean for the predictor. Conceptually, this is not at all similar to the centering options at level 2. When predictors are entered group-mean centered, this produces an analysis that is conceptually equivalent to conducting a separate regression analysis for each group and then treating the coefficients from those analyses as dependent measures in another analysis: hence the term "slopes as outcomes." In our example, if Ability was entered group-mean centered, then the intercept would represent the expected score in each classroom for a student of average ability, with "average" being defined in terms of all the students in his or her classroom.

Generally speaking, parameter estimates for intercepts vary more as a function of how predictors are centered than parameter estimates of slopes. When a predictor is entered group-mean centered, the estimate of the intercept for each group is basically the same as it was when there were no predictors. This means that the intercept of the intercept (γ_{00}) is pretty much unchanged from the unconditional model, aside from minor differences due to the estimation algorithm. This is because, similar to OLS regression, when predictors are entered group-mean centered, the outcome score for someone at the mean of a predictor is the mean outcome. Moreover, the level 2 variance of the intercept (the variance of μ_{0j}) is pretty much the same as it was in an unconditional model because the intercept has not changed.

In contrast, when a level 1 predictor is entered either uncentered or grand-mean centered, the intercept for each group may not be the same (actually, will probably not be the same) as the intercept from an unconditional model. In terms of our classroom example, the parameter estimates for the intercept (the mean and variance) of the expected classroom score for students who have no ability (which is what the intercept represents when Ability is entered uncentered) will probably be different than estimates of the expected classroom score for all students (the intercept from the unconditional model). Similarly, the parameter estimates for the intercept for students who have an ability level the same as the grand mean will also probably be different than estimates for all students.

One of the critical consequences of entering level 1 predictors grand-mean centered is that this adjusts the intercept for level 2 differences in the predictor, something that may be desirable or not. The potential importance of this difference is illustrated by example in the next section. Moreover, grand-mean centering a level 1 predictor brings level 2 variance into the level 1 model because deviations are being calculated based on the grand mean. If level 1 units do not vary at all in terms of the mean for a level 2 predictor (i.e., if all the group means are the same and therefore all are equal to the grand mean), then group- and grand-mean centering will produce exactly the same results. Given that this is pretty much never going to happen, group- and grand-mean centering level 1 predictors will produce different results, and how much they differ will vary as a function of how much the level 2 means of the level 1 predictors vary.

Recommendations: keeping in mind Bryk and Raudenbush's advice "That no single rule covers all cases," I recommend the following. At all levels of analysis, variables representing categorical predictors should be entered uncentered, unless there is a reason to adjust an intercept for the distribution of categories when using dummy codes. This makes it easier to generate predicted values to illustrate results. At level 2, continuous measures should be entered grand-mean centered, particularly if the scale has no valid zero-point. This also makes the coefficients easier to understand for those accustomed to OLS regression. Note that because a scale has a valid zero-point is not a sufficient justification to enter it uncentered, although the absence of a valid zero-point makes a good case for not entering a predictor uncentered.

At level 1, I recommend that in general, continuous measures should be entered group-mean centered. This eliminates the influence of level 2 differences in pre-dictors from an analysis. For example, assume a diary study in which some par-ticipants are depressed and some are not, and the focus is on individual differences in reactions to negative events, a "slopes as outcomes" analysis with daily self-esteem as the outcome (e.g., Nezlek & Gable, 2001). A simplified form of the models is:

$$y_{ij} = \beta_{0j} + \beta_{1j} \text{ (Negative Events)} + r_{ij}$$
$$\beta_{0j} = \gamma_{00} + \gamma_{01} \text{ (Depression)} + \mu_{0j}$$
$$\beta_{1j} = \gamma_{10} + \gamma_{11} \text{ (Depression)} + \mu_{1j}$$

If Negative Events were entered grand-mean centered at level 1, then individual differences in means of event scores (e.g., on average, depressed people report more negative events than those who are not depressed) would influence esti-mates of the within-person (level 1) relationship between self-esteem and events. Conceptually, and particularly because Depression was being entered as a level 2 predictor, we thought it best to control for individual differences in mean negative event scores; hence we group-mean centered event scores at level 1.

Some analysts (e.g., Kreft & de Leeuw, 1998) argue that when a predictor is entered group-mean centered, the mean of this predictor should be included as a level 2 predictor. The primary rationale for this is that when a level 1 predictor is entered group-mean centered, the level 2 variance of that predictor is eliminated from a model and such variance should be part of a model. On the other hand, other analysts (e.g., Bryk & Raudenbush) do not discuss this as a big problem and seem to be perfectly content to enter level 1 predictors group-mean centered without entering the mean at level 2. I tend to side with Bryk and Raudenbush on this issue, but analysts who are concerned about all this should run their models both ways and see what happens.

Contextual effects: an example of differences between group-mean and grand-mean centering

Although using different centering options at level 1 may not have important implications for the substantive conclusions indicated by a model, sometimes the differences are considerable and meaningful, and I illustrate this by a discussion of what multilevel modelers call a "contextual effect." To provide an example relevant to social and personality psychologists, I discuss contextual effects within the context of research on what is sometimes called the "Big Fish in a Little Pond Effect" (BFLPE). One conclusion of research on the BFLPE is that students' self-concept improves when they are placed in low ability classes or schools, or conversely, that their self-concept suffers when they are placed in high ability settings. Moreover, this effect has been described as robust across cultures and domains (e.g., Marsh & Hau, 2003). What is interesting about this relationship is that self-concept and ability tend to be positively related across virtually all domains and in virtually all cultures. More able students tend to have better self-concepts than less able students.

The critical support for the BFLPE comes from multilevel analyses in which a negative relationship is found between a level 2 variable such as class average ability (the average ability in a class based on standard tests) and the intercept from a level 1 model in which self-concept is the dependent measure and students' individual ability is the independent variable. The equations representing these analyses are presented below. There are i students nested within j classes whose ability and self-concept are measured. The critical coefficient is γ_{01}, which represents the relationship between class average ability and self-concept and which is invariably negative.

$$y_{ij} = \beta_{0j} + \beta_{1j} (\text{Student Ability}) + r_{ij}$$
$$\beta_{0j} = \gamma_{00} + \gamma_{01} (\text{Class-Average-Ability}) + \mu_{0j}$$
$$\beta_{1j} = \gamma_{10} + \gamma_{11} (\text{Class-Average-Ability}) + \mu_{1j}$$

The critical question at hand is, what does the intercept from the level 1 model, β_{0j}, represent? In most articles on the BFLPE, authors standardize (across an entire sample) various measures including student ability, the level 1 predictor. These predictors are then entered uncentered into models. As discussed in Chapter 4 in the section "Standardization," standardizing a level 1 predictor across a sample is the functional equivalent of grand-mean centering the predictor if the predictor is entered uncentered. That is, when scores are standardized they are transformed in terms of deviations from a mean; in the case of BFLPE research, this is the grand mean.

As explained above, when predictors are entered grand-mean centered, the intercept represents the expected score for an observation (in this case, a student) with a value at the grand mean of the predictor. In essence, the intercept for each group is adjusted for level 2 differences in the means of the predictors. In the case of research on the BFLPE, this means that the intercept for each class (β_{0j}) is the expected score for a student in the class who has the average level of ability, and "average" in this case refers to the overall (grand mean) average score of ability. The conclusion that students' self-concepts suffer when they are placed in high ability settings is based on the negative relationship between this "adjusted" intercept and the average class ability (the level 2 predictor). That is, the self-concept of a student with "average" ability (in terms of the overall population) is lower in classes of higher average ability than it is in classes of lower average ability.

It is important to note that if student ability is entered group-mean centered at level 1, the BFLPE disappears. When student ability is entered group-mean centered, the intercept represents the expected score for a student of average ability, with "average" defined in terms of the class in which the student is enrolled. Moreover, when ability is group-mean centered, the coefficient γ_{01} is no longer negative; in fact, it is positive.

I describe this situation not to criticize research on the BFLPE; rather, I describe it to highlight how results can vary as a function of different centering options. Whether group- or grand-mean centering is chosen, the mean within-class relationship between ability and self-concept is positive. In any class, more able students have higher self-concepts. Moreover, at the classroom level, the relationship between mean class self-concept and mean class ability is positive. Average self-concept tends to be higher in classes in which the average ability is higher compared to classes in which the average ability is lower.

The only negative relationship between ability and self-concept occurs when ability is a grand-mean centered predictor of self-concept at level 1, and the relationship between classroom average ability and the resulting adjusted intercept for self-concept is examined. This relationship has been used to support the contention that more able students have lower self-concepts in high ability classes than they should have (i.e., than they would have if classes were not divided by ability). The self-concept of a student of average ability is lower in high ability classes (or higher in lower ability classes) than would be expected from knowing only his or her ability. Centering can matter.

Modeling error

To me, modeling error terms in multilevel modeling is one of the most misunderstood (or poorly understood) aspects of the procedure. My sense is that many people assign too much importance to error terms when interpreting the results of their analyses. Much of this has to do with the fact that many people appear to assume that error terms in MLM are equivalent to error terms in OLS regression; however, there are important and meaningful differences between the two.

When thinking about how to model error in a multilevel model, it is important to think about the concepts underlying the analysis of a multilevel data structure. As I discussed at the outset, in a multilevel data structure there are multiple levels of sampling. For example, classrooms are sampled from the population of classrooms, and students in them are sampled from the population of students, and analyses that take into account the random sampling at all levels of analysis are more accurate than those that do not. One of the shortcomings of various types of OLS analyses that have been used to analyze multilevel data is that they do not take the random error at all levels of analysis into account; hence the superiority of MLM.

Moreover, unlike OLS analyses in which there is a single estimate of error, in MLM error terms can be estimated for each coefficient, and the covariances between these individual error terms can be estimated. Noting this, it may not always be possible to model (estimate) random error for all coefficients at all levels of analysis, but in all but the most unusual cases, the coefficients should be thought of as random and should be modeled as such if possible.

Within the terminology of MLM, two types of variance can be estimated for any coefficient – fixed and random. Fixed variance is used as the basis for conducting significance tests: is a coefficient significantly different from 0? Random variance is just that – random. The overwhelming and vast majority of hypotheses concern fixed effects. For example, is the relationship between studying and grades significantly different from 0? Is the relationship between stress and anxiety significantly different from 0? Testing such hypotheses has nothing to do with random error terms *per se*.

Nevertheless, the accuracy of the tests of the coefficients representing such relationships depends upon modeling error properly. One of the odd aspects of modeling error within MLM analyses is that it is difficult (if not impossible) to predict how improper modeling will affect the results of the tests of the fixed part of the coefficient – e.g., the coefficient representing the relationship between two variables. It is possible that the fixed part of a coefficient will be significantly different from 0 when the random effect is modeled, and it will not be significantly different when the random effect is not modeled. On the other hand, the fixed part of a coefficient may not be significant when the random error term is modeled, but it might be significant when it is not modeled. The only solution to this dilemma is to model error properly and then examine the fixed effects.

In my multilevel workshops, I use the following analogy. Think of error terms and structures as if they were the foundation of a house and think of the fixed effects as if they were the rooms in which you live. When buying a house, you want to know that the foundation is sound, but you do not buy a house because the foundation is good, you buy it because the rooms are pleasing. When "selling" your results to readers, readers are not going to "buy" what you have to say on the basis of how you model error because how you model error typically has nothing to do with your hypotheses *per se*. On the other hand, if you do not model error properly, readers may be unwilling to accept the results that pertain to your questions of interest; these results invariably concern the fixed effects because, if error is not modeled properly, the accuracy of the estimates of the fixed effects is suspect.

Within the multilevel framework, coefficients can be modeled in one of three ways: (1) with a random error term – sometimes referred to as randomly varying, (2) fixed – no random error term is estimated for a coefficient, and (3) non-randomly varying – discussed below. My recommendation is to model all effects as randomly varying at first and then delete random error terms from the model as need be.

MLM analyses rely on maximum likelihood estimates, and so the analyses are iterative. This is discussed later. Regardless, assuming the model you are running converges (or you tire of waiting and stop it from iterating), I recommend inspecting the error terms immediately, before examining the fixed effects. I recommend this because as noted above, improper error structures (what is technically called a mis-specified model) call into question the accuracy of the tests of the fixed effects. In MLM, all parameters are estimated simultaneously, so changes in the error structure can bring about changes in the tests of the fixed effects.

If all the error terms are significantly different from 0, then you are done and you can move on and examine the tests of the fixed effects. If they are not all significant, I recommend deleting those that are not significant and re-running the model. I recommend doing this because I (and others) see no sense in estimating something that cannot be estimated accurately. Estimating parameters requires information (data), and data structures contain a fixed amount of data. Analysts should use the data they have in the most efficient way possible, and it is simply not efficient to waste data on estimating something inaccurately. Noting all this, analysts should use a generous p-value (at least .10) when making decisions about retaining random error terms. Conceptually, most coefficients are random, and every effort should be made to model them as such.

Practically speaking, when I have a random error term that is on the cusp of significance (e.g., $p = .13$), I run the model with and without the random error term included and see what difference this makes. If the fixed effects are the same (more or less) in the two analyses, then I do not worry about whether the error term should be included. Its inclusion does not matter in terms of the coefficients that test my hypotheses – the fixed parts of the coefficients. On the other hand, if removing the random error term does matter, then I am more careful about estab-lishing a strict criterion for removing random error terms in all analyses, and I am more careful about applying this criterion uniformly. I will confess that I do not like it when significance tests of fixed effects vary as a function of the inclusion and exclusion of random error terms. It makes me think that the covariance matri-ces underlying the whole mess are not as stable as I want them to be. Nevertheless, you have to "play the hand you are dealt."

Some people assume that because a random error term is not estimated for a coefficient, then the coefficient does not vary. Although such coefficients are referred to as "fixed," such an assumption goes beyond what I think it should. When a random error term is not (or more accurately, cannot be) estimated for a coefficient, I think it is better to think of that coefficient as not randomly varying. When a random error term is not significant, this indicates that there is not enough information to provide an accurate and reliable estimate of the random variance of a coefficient. It does not indicate that the coefficient does not vary *per se*; rather, it indicates that there is not enough information to separate true and random variability.

Conceptualizing fixed effects this way becomes more understandable when one recognizes that differences in coefficients can be modeled even when no random error term is modeled for a coefficient. Such coefficients are referred to as non-randomly varying. For example, assume a study of work groups that has measured positive affect and attitudes toward the job at the individual worker level. When affect is modeled as a function of attitudes, the error term associated with the slope is not significant, $p = .5$, and so the error term is dropped. Despite this, group level differences in the slopes can still be modeled. A variable such as the nature of the type of task on which the group works could be included as a level 2 predictor of the slope representing the relationship between affect and attitudes.

When a random error term is not modeled, a coefficient is being held constant in the model for some purposes. Not estimating a random error term does not mean that a coefficient could not vary if the coefficient was modeled with a predictor. A non-significant random error term indicates that there is not enough information to model the variability of a coefficient without knowing more about the coefficient than the information contained in a model.

In the program HLM, the differences among coefficients that are modeled as randomly varying, fixed, and non-randomly varying can be seen by examining the contents of residual files. The following example is based upon data presented in Nezlek and Kuppens (2008). This study was a two-level design (days nested within persons). For this example, the outcome measure was daily self-esteem, and the predictor was the extent to which participants suppressed their negative emotions each day (negsupp). In Table 2, I present the first four cases from the residual files produced by various analyses. To create a residual file in the HLM program click on "Basic Settings" then "Level 2 Residual File." A thorough explanation of what is contained in residual files can be found by clicking on Help in the HLM program window.

$$y_{ij} = \beta_{0j} + \beta_{1j} \, (\text{negsupp}) + r_{ij}$$
$$\beta_{0j} = \gamma_{00} + \mu_{0j}$$
$$\beta_{1j} = \gamma_{10} + \mu_{1j}$$

The present example concerns a subset of the data in a level 2 residual file: the estimated Bayes (EB) residuals (variables that start with "eb"), the fitted values

Table 2   Contents of residual files

Panel 1 *Level 1 predictor random, no level 2 predictors*

fvintrcp	ebintrcp	ecintrcp	fvnegsup	ebnegsup	ecnegsup
5.522	−0.573	4.948	−0.049	−0.008	−0.057
5.522	0.547	6.068	−0.049	0.046	−0.004
5.522	−1.097	4.425	−0.049	−0.039	−0.089
5.522	0.877	6.399	−0.049	−0.213	−0.262

Panel 2 *Level 1 predictor fixed, no level 2 predictor*

fvintrcp	ebintrcp	ecintrcp	fvnegsup	ecnegsup
5.522	−0.572	4.950	−0.045	−0.045
5.522	0.545	6.067	−0.045	−0.045
5.522	−1.095	4.427	−0.045	−0.045
5.522	0.873	6.394	−0.045	−0.045

Panel 3 *Level 1 predictor fixed, sex as a level 2 predictor*

fvintrcp	ebintrcp	ecintrcp	fvnegsup	ecnegsup
5.555	−0.604	4.951	−0.006	−0.006
5.555	0.514	6.069	−0.006	−0.006
5.479	−1.054	4.425	−0.098	−0.098
5.479	0.913	6.393	−0.098	−0.098

Panel 4 *Level 1 predictor random, sex as a level 2 predictor*

fvintrcp	ebintrcp	ecintrcp	fvnegsup	ebnegsup	ecnegsup
5.555	−0.606	4.950	−0.013	−0.024	−0.037
5.555	0.515	6.070	−0.013	0.027	0.014
5.479	−1.056	4.423	−0.096	−0.016	−0.113
5.479	0.918	6.397	−0.096	−0.184	−0.281

(variables that start with "fv"), and the estimated Bayes coefficients (variables that start with "ec"). Measures of intercepts end with the letters "intrcp" and slopes end with the first six letters of the variable name ("negsup" in our example). So, fvintrcp is the fitted value for the intercept, ebintrcp is the estimated Bayes residual for the intercept, and ecintrcp is the estimated Bayes intercept. For ease of presentation, I did not include in the table coefficients describing OLS estimates and estimates of other measures. Note that estimated Bayes residuals are the data that are used to calculate random variation. When an effect is not modeled as random, no Bayes residual is estimated. For a more thorough explanation of Bayes residuals see Raudenbush and Bryk (2002).

In the first analyses (panel 1 in Table 2), both the intercept and the slope were modeled as randomly varying, and accordingly there was a level 2 error term for each, μ_{0j} and μ_{1j} respectively, and there were no level 2 predictors. Estimated Bayes coefficients are calculated by adding an EB residual to a corresponding fitted value. So, for case 1, the estimated intercept is 4.948 (−.573 + 5.522), and the estimated slope is −.057 (−.008 + (−.049)). For case 2, the estimated values are 6.068 (.547 + 5.522) and −.004 (.046 + (−.049)).

23

The second panel of data in Table 2 contains the residual file for a model in which the slope was modeled as fixed and the intercept was modeled as random (the level 2 equation for the slope is $\beta_{1j} = \gamma_{10}$). Estimated intercepts are calculated as they were above because the intercept is modeled as random. The critical difference between the two panels of data is that the estimated slope is the same for all level 2 units because no EB residual is estimated for fixed coefficients. The estimated slope is the fitted value, $-.045$. By the way, I did not delete the EB residual for the slope (ebnegsup) from the table; it was not included in the residual file. It is this lack of variability that leads people to believe that there is no variance in coefficient that is modeled without a random error term.

Technically speaking, when a coefficient is fixed and there is no level 2 predictor, no variance is being modeled; however, when a level 2 predictor is included, a different type of variance is being modeled. The third panel of data in Table 2 contains the residual file from a model in which the slope and intercept were modeled at level 2 as a function of a contrast-coded variable $(1, -1)$ representing the sex of the participant. The equations were $\beta_{0j} = \gamma_{00} + \gamma_{01}$ (Sex) and $\beta_{1j} = \gamma_{10} + \gamma_{10}$ (Sex). Similar to panel 2, the intercept was modeled as random, and the slope was modeled as fixed. The most important difference between panels 1 and 2 and panel 3 is the fitted values for both coefficients. In panel 3, the fitted values vary as a function of the level 2 predictor: for the intercept, the first two are 5.555, and the second two are 5.479; and for the slope, the first two are $-.006$ and the second two are $-.098$. If the level 2 predictor had been continuous, the fitted values would have taken on more than two values. Note that because the slope is fixed, there is not an EB residual, so the estimated slopes take on only two values.

Finally, panel 4 contains the residual file data from an analysis in which the intercept and slope were modeled as random and sex was included as a level 2 predictor for both coefficients. First, notice that the EB residual for the slope (ebnegsup) has reappeared because the slope is being modeled as random. The fitted values are also varying as a function of the level 2 predictor, and the estimated coefficients now reflect the contribution of the variance among the fitted values and the random variance of the coefficient.

I think of significance tests of random error terms as tests of one-sided hypotheses. If the random error term for a coefficient is significantly different from 0, an analyst can say that the coefficients vary. In contrast, if the random error term is not significant, a coefficient may still vary non-randomly as a function of level 2 differences. Given this, blanket statements such as "the coefficients are all the same because the random error term is not significant" need to be evaluated in light of the possibility that the coefficients may vary as a function of level 2 variables that have been collected.

Bottom line: do not over-interpret non-significant random error terms. In fact, I recommend specifying error terms properly and then more or less ignoring them. Most hypotheses concern the fixed effects. To return to the house analogy, build a solid foundation (your error structure), forget about it, and then relax in your living room (the fixed part of the coefficients). There will be more about error terms later when we consider building models.

Comparing coefficients

One of the most powerful features of MLM is the ability to compare coefficients, literally any coefficients or set of coefficients, in a model. How to do this using the program HLM is explained and illustrated in Chapter 5 on using HLM, but for various reasons it is important to describe the procedure here. The underlying rationale is to constrain a set of parameters to be equal (or to sum to 0: see section "Comparing the strength of coefficients with different signs" in Chapter 5), and to test how this constraint influences the fit of the model. If the constraint leads to a significantly poorer model then the comparison represented by constraint is significant.

As constraints, these are tested with χ^2 tests, with a degree of freedom for each comparison that is part of the constraint. I will illustrate this with the following example. Assume a level 1 model with three predictors. For present purposes, assume that all three predictors are in the same direction (positively related to the outcome).

$$y_{ij} = \beta_{0j} + \beta_{1j}(\text{Pred1}) + \beta_{2j}(\text{Pred2}) + \beta_{3j}(\text{Pred3}) + r_{ij}$$
$$\beta_{0j} = \gamma_{00} + \mu_{0j}$$
$$\beta_{1j} = \gamma_{10} + \mu_{1j}$$
$$\beta_{2j} = \gamma_{20} + \mu_{2j}$$
$$\beta_{3j} = \gamma_{30} + \mu_{3j}$$

One hypothesis posits that the relationship between y and Pred1 is stronger than the relationship between y and Pred2. This hypothesis can be tested by constraining the coefficients for Pred1 and Pred2 (γ_{10} and γ_{20}) to be equal, and the impact of such a constraint on the model would be tested with a 1 d.f. test. The hypothesis that Pred1 was different from Pred2 and Pred3 could also be tested with a 1 d.f. test (comparison of 2, −1, −1), with a 2 d.f. constraint (comparisons of 1, −1, 0 and 1, 0, −1), or with two 1 d.f. constraints (first comparison 1, −1, 0; second 1, 0, −1). Each of these options has advantages. The first and second options involve only one significance, test, whereas the third option involves two significance tests (one for each constraint); however, the third option provides the most detail. If either of the first two constraints is significant, it is still not certain if Pred1 is different from Pred2, or Pred1 is different from Pred3, or both.

The same techniques can also be used to test differences among coefficients representing level 2 predictors. For simplicity's sake, assume an unconditional level 1 model with three predictors at level 2 (L2A, L2B, L2C) that are all positively related to the outcome.

$$y_{ij} = \beta_{0j} + r_{ij}$$
$$\beta_{0j} = \gamma_{00} + \gamma_{01} (L2A) + \gamma_{02} (L2B) + \gamma_{03} (L2C) + \mu_{0j}$$

The hypothesis that the relationship between the outcome and L2A is stronger than the relationship between the outcome and L2B can be compared by constraining the γ_{01} and γ_{02} coefficients to be equal. Other comparisons among these coefficients can be tested using the same types of techniques that were discussed for comparing level 1 coefficients. Moreover, level 2 predictors can be added to level 1 models with multiple predictors (as in the previous example) and the strength of the cross-level relationships can be compared.

NB: the results of testing such constraints are not truly invariant under transformation. For example, the results of comparing L2A and L2B will vary if the variances of either is changed. In my experience, such differences are not pronounced, but they are not 0. This is one reason why in studies in which observations are nested within persons, I tend to standardize my level 2 measures; this eliminates any influence on the results that differences in the variances of level 2 measures may have. Also, at this point in time, I do not know of any studies that have examined the impact of multiple tests on type I error rates for these types of procedures. In own work, I have tended to use a series of pairwise comparisons because this provides the most detailed information – i.e., the ability to know where the significant differences are. I note, however, that I do this being mindful of the possibility that such procedures may inflate type I error rates.

Regardless, to me, such hypothesis testing is one of the "hidden gems" of MLM. Through the judicious use of coding and centering, analysts can estimate and compare coefficients representing very specific relationships or means. The secret behind using such comparisons is to understand and control exactly what each coefficient represents.

Categorical predictors and examining differences among groups: dummy codes and contrast codes

The preceding discussion has focused upon continuous measures as both dependent and independent variables. Nevertheless, analysts are frequently interested in categorical measures of either type. Categorical dependent measures require special techniques, and such analyses are described below. Here, I discuss the use of categorical predictors, and unlike categorical dependent measures, categorical independent measures (predictors) require no special treatment *per se*. They can be entered into a model at any level of analysis just as continuous predictors can be entered. For present purposes, I consider two types of categorical predictors, dummy coding and contrast coding.

Dummy-coded variables have only two values, 0 and 1. For example, I might represent participants' sex with a dummy-coded variable named Female. For female participants, the variable would take on a value of 1, and for male participants, it would take on a value of 0. In tandem, I might also generate a dummy-coded variable named Male. For female participants, the variable would take on a value of 0, and for male participants, it would take on a value of 1. Moreover, there are certain analyses that require such complementary coding schemes, and it is probably better to calculate a dummy code representing each category of a classification system at the same time.

Contrast-coded variables can take on different values depending upon the number of categories they represent and the comparisons among these categories they are intended to instantiate. For example, participant sex could be represented by a contrast code of +1 for females and −1 for males, or conversely, −1 for females and +1 for males. Note that there is no statistical difference between these two coding schemes: both will produce exactly the same results in terms of variance estimates and significance tests, but the signs of the coefficients will be reversed. In such situations, I choose the code that corresponds most closely to my expectations or hypotheses. To continue the example, if I think that women will have a higher mean than men will have, I will code female = +1. In this way, a positive coefficient represents confirmation of my hypotheses. No matter, use a coding system that makes sense to you and that you can explain to others.

Now comes the fun part. By combining centering options and coding schemes and following this with tests of fixed effects (see the previous section on comparing coefficients), it is possible to estimate means for different categories of observations (at either level) and to compare the differences between or among these means. Assume we have a study of performance with people nested within groups, and there are men and women in each group. If we wanted to estimate the differences between men and women, we could enter a contrast variable at level 1 (Sex-Cnt), and then analyze sex differences at level 2 as a function of the sexism of the group leader. The level 1 model would be:

$$y_{ij} = \beta_{0j} + \beta_{1j} \text{(Sex-Cnt)} + r_{ij}$$
$$\beta_{0j} = \gamma_{00} + \gamma_{01} \text{(Sexism)} + \mu_{0j}$$
$$\beta_{1j} = \gamma_{10} + \gamma_{11} \text{(Sexism)} + \mu_{1j}$$

At level 1, Sex-Cnt is entered uncentered, which means that the intercept represents the performance of neither men nor women. At level 2, Sexism is entered grand-mean centered. In such an analysis, if the γ_{10} coefficient is significantly different from 0 you would conclude that on average, men and women performed differently. If the γ_{11} coefficient was significantly different from 0, you could conclude that the sexist beliefs of the group leader were related to sex differences in performance.

A slightly different approach to this issue would be to examine if a leader's sexism was related in different ways to the performance of men versus women. Such a question could not be directly answered using a contrast variable. To do this, the performance of men and women have to be estimated separately. One, rather inelegant, solution to this would be to run two analyses, one with a dummy code at level 1 representing whether people were men, and another with a dummy code at level 1 representing whether people were women. By entering these dummy codes uncentered, the intercept would represent the expected value for when the dummy code is 0, and these intercepts could be brought up to level 2. The intercept in the following analyses would represent the performance of women, i.e., when Male = 0.

$$y_{ij} = \beta_{0j} + \beta_{1j} \text{ (Male)} + r_{ij}$$

Nevertheless, such analyses would not provide a basis to compare relationships between sexism and performance for men and women, at least not statistically. Moreover, estimating these two means separately (i.e., without the variance of both in the model simultaneously) is not as desirable as an analysis that estimates them simultaneously.

The best way to determine if a leader's sexism was related in different ways to the performance of men and women is to conduct an analysis with a no-intercept level 1 model with both the Male and Female dummy codes. The intercept is dropped from the analyses (note that the subscripts for coefficients start at 1 not 0), and the dummy codes are entered uncentered. If the intercept is not dropped or the dummy codes are centered in some way, the model will not run.

$$y_{ij} = \beta_{1j} \text{ (Male)} + \beta_{2j} \text{ (Female)} + r_{ij}$$
$$\beta_{1j} = \gamma_{10} + \gamma_{11} \text{ (Sexism)} + \mu_{1j}$$
$$\beta_{2j} = \gamma_{20} + \gamma_{21} \text{ (Sexism)} + \mu_{2j}$$

The fact that this analysis estimates means for women and men can be understood by noting that, for men, the β_{2j} is multiplied by 0 because Female = 0, whereas β_{1j} is multiplied by 1 because Male = 1. Therefore, β_{2j} drops out, and so the expected value for men equals β_{1j}. A parallel process occurs for women: Male = 0, Female = 1, and so β_{1j} drops out. Differences in the strength of the relationship between sexism and performance can be tested by constraining the γ_{11} and γ_{21} coefficients to be equal. If the constraint leads to a poorer fit, then the relationships are said to differ.

The intercepts (γ_{10} and γ_{20}, representing the mean performance of men and women respectively) can also be compared using such constraints. This begs the question about the difference between comparing categories (e.g., men v. women) by estimating separate means via dummy codes and comparing groups using contrast codes. (Well, it begged the question for me.) Typically, the estimate of the differences between categories and the results of the significance tests of such differences (the χ^2 for the constraint using the dummy codes and a t-test of the contrast coefficient) will be very (very) similar, although they will not be exactly the same. When using a contrast code you are estimating a score for each group that represents the difference between categories and testing if the mean difference score is different from 0. When using dummy codes, you are estimating two means (one for each category) for each group and testing if the means of these means are different.

In my experience, if your primary concern is simply testing differences between means, either method is fine – they are more less interchangeable. The type of analysis you do is determined by what you want to "bring up" to level 2. If you are interested in examining relationships between level 2 variables and some type of level 1 difference, use contrast codes. If you are interested in knowing if relationships between level 2 variables and a level 1 variable vary across level 1 categories, then use dummy codes.

The same logic and types of analyses can also be applied when you have more than two categories. With three categories you would need three dummy codes, with four you would need four, and so forth. Moreover, you can compare individual categories (either one-on-one or in combinations) using the tests of fixed effects described above. An important precondition for such analyses is that the categories are mutually exclusive. If there is any overlap (i.e., an observation has more than one dummy code that is 1), the parameter estimates will be invalid. Moreover, if you do not include all the dummy codes, be certain to keep clear what your intercepts and slopes represent. For example, if you have three categories and you include only the dummy codes for categories 2 and 3, you should not drop the intercept. The intercept will now represent the mean for category 1, and the slopes will represent the difference between categories 1 and 2 and categories 1 and 3 respectively.

For the contrast codes, you need to represent the contrast in which you are interested, under the constraint that the codes sum to 0. For example, for four groups, codes of -1, -1 and $+1$, $+1$ would compare the mean for groups 1 and 2 to the mean of groups 3 and 4. Once again, keep in mind that the contrast codes estimate a difference score at level 1 that is then brought up to level 2.

The same procedures can be used to examine differences among categories at level 2. A series of dummy or contrast codes can be used to represent the categories in which level 2 observations can be placed, and when using dummy codes, the estimates for individual categories can be compared using tests of fixed effects. Just keep in mind that (as described below) you should have the same level 2 mode for each level 1 coefficient.

Building a model

As a general rule, multilevel modelers recommend starting with what is typically called an "unconditional" or "null" model, and this can be considered as a preliminary, descriptive analysis. In fact, the results of unconditional models provide the basic descriptive statistics for a multilevel data structure: the mean and the variances at different levels. In such models, there are no predictors at any level of analysis. Although such analyses rarely test hypotheses *per se*, they provide valuable information about the distribution of variance in a measure, and by extension, they provide a hint about "where the action is" in a data set – i.e., the levels of analysis at which analyses might be the most productive. See analyses of the example data set in Chapter 5 on using HLM.

If there is no or little variance at a particular level of analysis, it may be difficult to find relationships at that level of analysis. For example, in Nezlek, Kafetsios, and Smith (2008), a social interaction diary study focusing on emotions in interaction, the person level variances of measures of negative affect were much lower than the person level variances of measures of positive affect. In fact, for some measures of negative affect, less than 10% of the total variability was at the person level. The hypotheses and analyses focused on relationships between self-construal and mean affect (person level relationships), and so it was not surprising that we found no significant relationships between self-construal and negative affect. In contrast, there was meaningful person level variance in the measures of positive affect, and we found numerous relationships between self-construal and positive affect.

As a bit of a cautionary note, I will confess that I did not follow my own advice when doing the analyses for that paper. I did not run unconditional models, and in the first drafts of the paper, my colleagues and I found it difficult to explain why we had pretty sensible results for our measures of positive affect but nothing sensible for negative affect. For whatever reasons, we ran some unconditional models and looked at the variance distributions. Mystery over. Physician, heal thyself.

On the other hand, note that I said that unconditional models provide a hint about the levels at which analyses might be productive, and in this circumstance, hints are just hints – suggestions about how to proceed. For example, in Matsumoto, Nezlek, and Koopman (2007), a cross-cultural study in which persons were nested within countries, some of the hypotheses and analyses concerned country level (level 2) relationships between Hofstede's measures of cultural orientation and measures of various aspects of emotional expression and experience. For virtually all of the individual level measures of emotion, there was very little variance at the between-country level (level 2) – less than 10% for most measures. Such a distribution did not bode well for finding relationships at the country level. Nevertheless, we found numerous significant relationships between country level means and Hofstede's measures.

Bottom line: let the variance distributions provided by unconditional models inform and guide you, but do not let them limit you.

After you get acquainted with your data, most multilevel modelers recommend that you build your level 1 model first. This entails adding predictors of interest and settling upon an error structure – i.e., deciding which effects will be random and which will need to be fixed. Do not be surprised if significance levels of random effects change as a function of the specific level 1 predictors that are in a model. Remember, random effects are estimates based upon covariance matrices, and adding or deleting variables changes covariance matrices, which can lead to changes in the estimates of individual parameters such as random error terms.

In my experience, it is not uncommon to have a few predictors (say four) and to find some of the random error terms (say two of four) are not significant. Yet, when I fix one of the coefficients that has a non-significant random error term, the random error term for another effect that was not significant becomes significant. Moreover, it is sometimes the case that such changes can go either way.

Assume variables A and B both have non-significant random error terms: there is not enough information in the data to estimate reliably these error terms and their covariances with other random error terms. It is possible that fixing variable A makes the random term for variable B significant, and fixing variable B makes the random error term for variable A significant. What to do? Which one should be fixed? There is no clear guidance for such cases. When I am faced with such a situation, I fix the term that is the weakest using p-levels when all coefficients are modeled as random. I am also influenced by the importance (to the question at hand) of the measure and the relative value conceptually of modeling one coefficient as random versus modeling the other as random.

Once this is all straight, then level 2 predictors are added depending upon your hypotheses and questions of interest. It may happen that a random error term that was significant without any level 2 predictors in a model becomes non-significant when level 2 predictors are added. In such cases I recommend deleting non-significant random error terms just as I recommended above. Is the reverse possible? Can a non-significant random error term become significant when a level 2 predictor is added? Yes, although this rarely happens. When it does, I recommend retaining error terms that are significant. Nevertheless, when there is any doubt about the inclusion or exclusion of random error terms, models can be run with and without the terms to see what effect this has on the other parameters (e.g., fixed effects) estimated by the model.

There are times when it is quite obvious that no matter what is added to or taken from a model, a random error term is not going to be significant – e.g., the p-level of the test is hovering around .5 to .8. There are also times when it is just as obvious that a random error term is going to remain significant no matter what is added to or taken from a model. In other cases, the possibility that significance levels of random error terms will change as a function of adding predictors may not be so easy to determine without making the changes and seeing what happens.

As a back-up position, you can always run models with different error structures and see how the fixed parts of coefficients vary as a function of how error is modeled. If the fixed effects do not vary, the selection of error structures becomes largely an academic issue (no pun intended). As noted above, if a fixed effect starts to vary meaningfully as a function of changes in error structures, one needs to be cautious when interpreting the results.

Finally, it is also possible to evaluate the appropriateness of different error structures by comparing model fits. In MLM, model fits are represented by what is called a deviance statistic. The fits of models with the same fixed components but different error structures can be compared using the deviance statistics associated with each model. This can be particularly useful when numerous error terms have been deleted sequentially on a case-by-case basis. The important difference between evaluating error structures by comparing deviance statistics of models and making decisions about error terms individually is that model comparisons take into account the covariances of error terms with each other, whereas significance tests of individual terms do not.

I will not dwell any more on random error terms. As I said earlier, they are invariably not related to the hypotheses posed by the majority of personality and social psychologists. Nevertheless, they can be confusing and analysts should understand what they are doing and why, and zealous reviewers and editors sometimes insist on knowing the details of this aspect of MLM.

Adding variables to a regression equation is often referred to as "stepping," and there are primarily two forms of stepping, forward and backward. Forward stepping refers to adding predictors to an existing model, sometimes one at a time, sometimes in groups. Backward stepping refers to adding many predictors at the outset and then deleting some based on the significance tests of individual coefficients, sometimes one at a time, sometimes in groups.

Many analysts whose primary experience is OLS regression are accustomed to backward-stepping procedures. I refer to this as the "soldier of fortune" approach: Kill 'em all and let God sort them out. You include a bunch of predictors and see which ones are significant. Although backward stepping may be a reasonable approach when an analyst has a lot of cases, it is not the best way to build a model within the multilevel framework, particularly at level 1 in a two-level model (or at levels 1 and 2 in a three-level model).

Most multilevel modelers recommend forward stepping. An important reason for this is the difference in the number of parameters estimated by MLM in comparison to OLS regression. In OLS regression, you estimate an intercept, a coefficient for each predictor, and an error term. For a level 1 model in MLM you estimate an intercept, a coefficient for each predictor, an error term for each predictor, the covariances among these error terms, and a level 1 error term.

In addition to the level 1 error term, starting with the basic level 1 model, $y_{ij} = \beta_{0j} + r_{ij}$, two parameters are estimated, a fixed and a random term for the intercept (γ_{00} and μ_{0j}). When a predictor is added, $y_{ij} = \beta_{0j} + \beta_{1j}(x) + r_{ij}$, a total of five additional parameters are estimated: fixed and random terms for the intercept and the slope (γ_{00}, μ_{0j}, and γ_{10}, μ_{1j}), and the covariance between the two random terms. When a second predictor is added, $y_{ij} = \beta_{0j} + \beta_{1j}(x_1) + \beta_{2j}(x_2) + r_{ij}$, the model estimates nine additional parameters: fixed and random terms for the intercept and the two slopes (total of six), and the covariances between the three random terms (three). As can be seen from this simple example, the number of parameters estimated in a MLM analysis increases non-linearly as a function of the number of level 1 predictors. In contrast, in OLS regression, each additional predictor adds only one new parameter regardless of how many predictors there were in the previous model.

The observations that comprise a data set are information, and it takes information to estimate parameters. Some statisticians use the term "carrying capacity" to describe a data set's ability to estimate parameters. More data (observations) provide more carrying capacity – i.e., the ability to estimate more parameters more accurately. If too many predictors are added, the carrying capacity of a data set may be exceeded, and the accuracy of the estimated parameters will be compromised. This will be apparent when random error terms cannot be estimated, when models take an excessive number of iterations to converge, and so forth. The norm among multilevel modelers is to build "tight" models – parsimonious models with the fewest predictors possible, with the most accurate parameter estimates possible. Less is more.

Finally, as discussed in Chapter 4 in the section "Reporting guidelines," I do not recommend presenting sequential tests of models based on model fits (deviance statistics). First, comparing models that differ in terms of the fixed effects (i.e., differences in predictors) requires full maximum likelihood estimators rather than the more accurate (in terms of estimating individual coefficients) restricted maximum likelihood estimators. Second, such overall comparisons include both the fixed and the random (error) structures, and typically, hypotheses do not concern the various components of the error structure. Less detail is more informative.

Diagnostics

In my experience, the three most common problems people have in getting their multilevel models to "work", are data preparation, model specification in terms of the fixed components, and model specification in terms of the random components. At the most basic level, as discussed in Chapter 5, when using the program HLM, people may have trouble creating the MDM file, which is the save file or system file HLM uses as a basis for analyses. More often than not, this is due to sorting errors. For programs in which data from different levels need to be duplicated and appended, analysts need to be certain that this has been done properly. Nothing succeeds like simple visual inspection of files. With experience, such problems tend to diminish, but it is amazing how often they can reappear.

Assuming the data have been prepared properly, a model may not run because of problems with the fixed part of the model. The term "fixed part" refers to the predictors that are entered at the various levels of analysis. Problems with the fixed part typically result from linear dependence among a set of predictors. For example, assume that at some level of the design there are three groups (or categories), each of which is represented by a dummy-coded variable. If all three dummy codes are included in a model and the intercept is not removed, the analysis will "crash" because of the linear dependence among these predictors. Note the emphasis on the inclusion of the intercept. As explained earlier in this chapter in the section on analyzing differences among groups, it is possible to include dummy codes representing all the groups at a level of analysis if the intercept is removed.

By far, the most common problem people have getting multilevel analyses to work has to do with estimating random errors and their covariances. This is typically indicated by the fact that an analysis requires an excessive number of iterations to converge. As noted above, programs that perform MLM analyses use algorithms to estimate parameters. These algorithms are iterative in that a set of parameters and an accompanying model fit are estimated, changes are made to these parameters, and the model fit of this new set of parameters is compared to the fit of the previous set. The analysis is done when the difference between model n and model $n - 1$ becomes small enough. This cut-off is called the convergence criterion, and as mentioned below, it is something that can be changed by an analyst.

Generally speaking, multilevel modelers like it when their models converge quickly, i.e., the difference in the fits of models n and $n - 1$ becomes small in relatively few iterations. Although it might be difficult to get someone to commit to a hard and fast definition of "relatively few," my guess is that these days anything less than a few hundred iterations would qualify as relatively few. I will note that with the advent of low cost, high speed computing, the number of iterations is probably not as important to many analysts as it was in the past. Nevertheless, models that take many iterations to converge may have some problems or weaknesses.

When an analysis takes an excessive number of iterations to converge, this invariably reflects difficulty in estimating one or more random error terms and/or the covariances between random errors. Technically speaking, the estimation algorithm often encounters what are called "local minima." The algorithm changes the estimate of a parameter (or parameters) to improve the fit, but because one or more parameters cannot be estimated, the fit never changes – i.e., the model does not converge.

Generally, this is not a cause for alarm. Most programs print the error terms (and the significance tests for them) and the error covariance matrices. Simple visual inspection can identify the culprit(s), and the problematic error terms can be eliminated (see previous discussion on modeling error). In rare instances (at least rare in my experience), difficulties in convergence will reflect difficulties in estimating a covariance between two error terms. Some programs such as MLwiN allow analysts to fix elements of an error covariance matrix to a specific value, whereas others such as HLM do not. In HLM, when an error term is estimated, the covariances between that error term and all other error terms will be estimated. For my purposes, I have not found it necessary to delve into the elements of error covariance matrices, but some analysts might. Another hint that an error term is responsible for convergence problems can be found by examining reliability estimates. As noted in the earlier section on "Modeling error," low reliabilities indicate that the program has had difficulty separating true from random variability.

3

Multilevel Random Coefficient Models: Some Advanced Topics

Using residual variances

As discussed previously, understanding random error terms (sometimes referred to as residual error) can be challenging within the multilevel context, particularly for analysts who think of MLM in terms of OLS analyses. Such challenges are particularly salient when trying to estimate variance accounted for, or variance reductions, or when using variances to estimate effect sizes. When thinking of residual variances in MLM I keep in mind the following recommendation of Kreft and de Leeuw: "In general, we suggest not setting too much store by the calculation of R^2_B [level 2 variance] or R^2_W [level 1 variance]" (1998: 119).

In this section, I describe the important factors that I think need to be considered when using residual variances to estimate outcomes of an analysis. It is important to note that this is a topic about which there is probably no consensus and about which well-intentioned and intelligent authors may disagree. Perhaps a consensus may emerge in the future.

First, keep in mind that variance estimates are not available unless a random error term is estimated for a coefficient. Although, as mentioned earlier, you can model differences in coefficients even when a random error term is not estimated, for purposes of estimating variances, a random error term needs to be estimated. This is one of the limitations of using variance estimates for any purpose within the multilevel framework.

Second, individual coefficients have their own error terms. In OLS terms, each level 1 coefficient can be thought of as having its own equation at level 2. Although it is possible to evaluate the improvement that adding a variable makes to a model through comparisons of deviance statistics, such improvements are not the same as reductions in variance. For example, as measures of total model fit, deviance statistics include error terms and their covariances.

Third, to avoid introducing level 2 variance into the calculation of level 1 variances, level 1 predictors must be entered group-mean centered. However appropriate they may be for other purposes, grand-mean and zero centered predictors introduce level 2 differences in level 1 predictors, reducing the validity of estimates of level 1 residual variances.

Fourth, and somewhat counterintuitive for OLS users, adding a significant predictor to a multilevel model may not change residual variance estimates. Within OLS regression, significance tests of predictors are based upon changes in residual variance estimates. If adding a predictor does not reduce the residual variance of a model (or if deleting one does not increase the residual variance) then the predictor is not significant. In contrast, in MLM, significant predictors can be added to a model with no change in residual variances. In my experience, this has been much more of a problem at level 1 than at level 2, but I urge analysts to be cautious in general.

In OLS analyses, significance tests of fixed effects and variances are estimated simultaneously. The variance is based solely on deviations from the mean. The maximum likelihood algorithms used by MLM programs estimate fixed effects and random terms separately (or in separate parts of the algorithm), so a change in the fixed part of the model may not be accompanied by a change in the random part of the model.

With these important caveats in mind, within the multilevel framework error variances can be treated in a fashion similar to how they are treated within the OLS framework. For example, effect sizes can be estimated by taking the difference between the residual variances of two models and dividing it by the residual variance of the first model. Similarly, relationships can be expressed as correlations – square roots of the percentage of reductions in variance. In my own multilevel work, I am cautious about estimating effect sizes using residual variances because of the caveats I described above, and when I present effect sizes I mention these caveats. Nevertheless, when a model with only one predictor is being compared to a model with no predictors, difficulties such as those described above with adding significant predictors that do not reduce residual variances cannot occur.

Interactions

Within the multilevel context, there are two types of interactions, within-level and between-level (also referred to as cross-level). Both are interactions in the sense that an interaction is said to exist when the relationship between two variables varies as a function of a third variable. In the case of cross-level interactions, a relationship at one level of analysis varies as a function of a variable at another level of analysis. In a two-level data structure, a cross-level interaction occurs when a relationship between two level 1 variables varies as a function of a level 2 variable. For example, in a daily diary study, the relationship between daily stress and daily affect (level 1) might vary as a function of a trait level measure such as neuroticism (level 2). In a study in which students are nested within classes, the relationship between students' grades and the amount they studied (level 1) might vary as a function of teachers' experience (level 2). Similarly, in a three-level model, a level 2 relationship might vary as a function of a level 3 variable. Cross-level interactions are also referred to as "slopes as outcomes" analyses because slopes from level 1 become (conceptually) outcomes (dependent variables) at level 2. Such analyses are also sometimes referred to as moderated relationships because a level 1 relationship is described as varying as a function of (or being moderated by) a level 2 variable.

In HLM, cross-level interactions can be created and tested by the program itself. In terms of the HLM interface, a variable is entered at level 1 as a predictor, and then a level 2 variable is entered as a predictor in the equation for the slope (the coefficient representing the relationship between the two level 1 variables). This procedure is discussed below in detail. In other programs, cross-level interactions are created and tested in different ways, and analysts are encouraged to consult relevant manuals carefully for the appropriate set of commands.

Keep in mind that it is possible to examine such cross-level interactions (or moderating relationships) even when the mean level 1 slope is not significantly different from 0. For example, in a diary study, the mean relationship between an outcome (e.g., mood) and a predictor (e.g., type of event) might be 0. Nevertheless, for some people the relationship might be positive, whereas for others it might be negative, a situation that could produce a mean that was not significantly different from 0. If this were the case, it might be possible to model the differences in slopes, i.e., to determine for whom the slope was positive and for whom it was negative. Similarly, in a study in which persons were nested within groups, the relationship between two variables (e.g., productivity and time on the job) might be negative for some groups and positive for others. The mean relationship might be 0, but it still might be possible to model these differences and determine the types of groups in which the relationship is positive, and the types in which it is negative.

Within-level interactions can be more complicated to set up and more complicated to interpret than between-level interactions. At the top level in a data structure (e.g., level 2 in a two-level model and level 3 in a three-level model), creating interaction terms is straightforward and follows guidelines and conventions that are indistinguishable from those used to create interaction terms in OLS regression. See Aiken and West (1991) for a thorough discussion of interaction within a regression framework. Continuous variables can be mean centered (the mean is subtracted from individual values), and the resulting mean centered variables can be multiplied by each other or by variables representing different groups, and so forth. In terms of how such interaction terms should be centered when entering them into a model, I recommend adding interaction terms uncentered because the variables that are used to create interaction terms have been centered before the terms have been created. Moreover, entering interaction terms uncentered eases the all-important estimation of predicted values – see below.

At level 1 in both two- and three-level data structures and at level 2 in a three-level data structure, creating within-level interaction terms is conceptually similar to what was just described but is a little more complicated. To provide the "purest" estimate of the interaction I recommend centering measures around the mean for each group at a level of analysis. For example, in a two-level study in which students are nested within classes, a mean score should be calculated for each classroom and the difference between each student's score and the mean score for his or her classroom is calculated. In a two-level daily diary study, a mean daily response should be calculated for each person and the difference between each day's score and the mean score for each person should be calculated. These scores are then multiplied by other variables of interest, and the product is entered uncentered into the model. I recommend entering continuous measures that are involved in an interaction group-mean centered to avoid introducing level 2 variance into the level 1 interaction term. In a three-level model (e.g., occasions nested within days and days nested within persons), interactions at level 1 would be calculated by calculating an average score within each day within each person and subtracting that mean from the score for each occasion. The level 2 (day level) interactions should be calculated as described above and entered uncentered.

My conceptual goal in advocating these procedures is to maximize the similarity between a formal MLM and simply doing a bunch of regression analyses (one for each group, classroom, or person) and using the coefficients from such analyses in other analyses. If continuous measures are mean centered and then multiplied as described above and the predictors themselves are entered group-mean centered (as advocated earlier), entering the interaction term uncentered means that the interaction term represents the expected value for an observation that has a 0 interaction (i.e., no interaction). If the interaction term is entered centered (somehow), the interaction term needs to be evaluated in terms of the mean interaction terms (either group mean or grand mean). To me, it is much easier to use 0 as a reference point, and 0 has the advantage of being substantively meaningful (i.e., no interaction).

What is critically important (and what can be cumbersome) is generating predicted values to interpret interactions. I recommend estimating values for cases that are 1 SD above and below the mean, the standard approach recommended by most regression analysts. For interactions at the "highest" level of analysis (e.g., level 2 in a two-level model and level 3 in a three-level model) such estimation is pretty straightforward, and follows standard OLS procedures. Scores for the predictors representing ±1 SD are multiplied by the coefficients, and predicted outcomes are estimated.

Generating predicted values to describe within-level interactions at lower levels of analysis (e.g., level 1 within a two-level model and levels 1 and 2 within a three-level model) is a bit more complicated. The most important aspect of this is to estimate the within-level SD properly. The within-level SD is not the SD produced by a simple descriptive analysis of a variable from a "flat file" – a file that does not take the multilevel structure of the data into account. Variance estimates from flat files combine variances from all levels of analysis. Within-level SDs need to be taken from unconditional models of a variable. For a two-level model, the level 1 SD is the square root of the level 1 variance from an unconditional model, and for a three-level model, the level 1 and 2 SDs can be estimated from the level 1 and 2 variances respectively.

An example of this procedure can be found in Nezlek and Plesko (2003: 589–590). In this study, we examined the buffering effect – the possibility that daily negative events have less of an impact on daily well-being when there are more daily positive events than when there are fewer positive events, a within-person (within-level) interaction. The within-person SDs for event scores were based on unconditional analyses of the event scores (see Table 1 in Nezlek & Plesko, 2003), and predicted values (Table 3) were generated using the coefficients presented in Table 2. The model is below. Note that there is no error term for the interaction coefficient. It was not significant in any of the analyses.

$$y_{ij} = \beta_{0j} + \beta_{1j} (\text{Pos}) + \beta_{2j} (\text{Neg}) + \beta_{3j} (\text{Pos-Neg}) + r_{ij}$$
$$\beta_{0j} = \gamma_{00} + \mu_{0j}$$
$$\beta_{1j} = \gamma_{10} + \mu_{1j}$$
$$\beta_{2j} = \gamma_{20} + \mu_{2j}$$
$$\beta_{3j} = \gamma_{30}$$

One key component of generating these predicted values that was not discussed in the article was how to generate the values for the interaction term that were then "plugged into" the prediction equation. To recap, in this study, the SD for positive events was .48, and it was .40 for negative events. So, for a day that was +1 SD on positive events and +1 SD on negative events, the value to "plug into" the prediction equation would be .48 × .40 = +.192. For a day that was +1 SD on positive events and −1 SD on negative events, the value to "plug into" the prediction equation for the interaction term (Pos-Neg) would be .48 × −.40 = −.192. Similarly, −1 SD positive and +1 SD negative would be −.48 × .40 = −.192; and −1 SD positive and −1 SD negative would be −.48 × −.40 = +.192.

Let's generate predicted values for the "triad" measure (a daily measure of well-being based on Beck's triad; more details are given in Chapter 5, "Using HLM"). The coefficients were: intercept, 5.10; positive events, .75; negative events, −.81; and interaction term, .25. In the tabulation are shown the equations with substituted values to generate predicted values for four different days, a combination of high and low positive and negative events. When positive events are high, the contribution of positive event is +.48 × .75 = .36. When they are low, it is −.48 × .75 = −.36. When negative events are high, the contribution is .40 × −.81 = −.32. When they are low, it is −.40 × −.81 = +.32. The contribution of the interaction term is calculated by multiplying the appropriate value (discussed in the previous paragraph) by .25, the coefficient for the interaction term.

Positive events	Negative events	Predicted	Intercept	Positive events	Negative events	Interaction
High	High	5.18	5.10	+.36	−.32	+.048
High	Low	5.72	5.10	+.36	+.32	−.048
Low	High	4.39	5.10	−.36	−.32	+.048
Low	Low	5.11	5.10	−.36	+.32	−.048

As explained in the article, the buffering effect is the extent to which the impact of negative events varies as a function of the level of positive events. For these data, that was estimated as follows:

5.72 − 5.18 = .54 (impact on high positive days) versus

5.11 − 4.39 = .72 (impact on low positive days) leads to

buffering effect .72 − .54 = .18; for everything else, there's MasterCard

If that is not enough for you, in the article we also reported the results of how this buffering effect varied as a function of trait level (level 2) differences such as depression. This was done by adding a level 2 predictor such as scores on the Center for Epidemiological Center Depression scale (CESD; Radloff, 1977) to each of the level 2 equations in the model described above. These analyses found that, in some cases, the buffering effect (the level 1 interaction between positive and negative events) varied as a function of level 2 individual differences, e.g., the CESD moderated the buffering effect described above. Estimating predicted values to illustrate this moderating effect is a two-stage process.

First, sets of coefficients (intercept and slopes) are estimated for people ±1 SD on the CESD. Assuming the CESD was entered grand-mean centered (or was standardized prior to analysis), there is no need to estimate a set of coefficients for people at the mean: these are the coefficients produced by the original analysis without the CESD as a predictor. The coefficients for the level 2 moderators are presented in Table 6 of the article. For the triad and CESD, they were −.54, .23, .01, and .24 for the intercept, positive events, negative events, and interaction terms respectively. The trait level measures were standardized prior to analysis, so coefficients for people high on the CESD could be generated by adding the moderating coefficient to the original (a score of 1.0 on the CESD represents 1 SD). Applying these moderating coefficients to the original coefficients of 5.10, .75, −.81, and .25 produces the following sets of coefficients. For those high on the CESD the coefficients are 4.56, .98, −.80, and .49. For those low on the CESD, the coefficients are 5.64, .42, −.82, and .01. Note that the buffering effect is pretty much 0 for those low on the CESD.

The second step is to estimate predicted values for days high and low in positive and negative events for people low and high on the CESD. This is done using the same procedures described for the overall analyses. The same SDs are used, but the estimated values are calculated using the coefficients for people who are high or low on the CESD. For example, for people high on the CESD, the contribution of positive events is ±.47 (.48 × .98), the contribution of negative events is ±.32 (.40 × .80), and the contribution of the interaction is ±.094 (.192 × .49). These contributions are then added or subtracted from the intercept for people low on the CESD (4.56) to generate predicted values for the four types of days (the combination of low–high and positive–negative events). The same process is then applied to generate coefficients and predicted values for people low on the CESD for the four types of days.

Admittedly, this is a lot of estimation and calculation, but think of the fact that these numbers are describing how a within-person interaction is moderated by a between-person difference. That is a mouthful. Practically speaking, I tend to use Excel to set up all these coefficients and estimated values. You can enter the coefficients once, plug some values into the cells, and off you go.

Moderation and mediation

When discussing moderation and mediation, I will rely on the classic distinction discussed by Baron and Kenny (1986). Broadly speaking, moderation exists when a relationship between two variables (e.g., x and y) varies as a function of a third variable (e.g., z). Within the multilevel framework, moderation is represented by interactions, a representation that is conceptually similar to the OLS framework. Across levels of analysis, this occurs when a level 1 relationship varies as a function of a level 2 variable. In such cases, the level 2 variable is described as moderating the level 1 relationship. Moderating relationships can also exist among variables within a level of analysis, as represented by the within-level interactions discussed above, and depending how a model is up, one variable can be described as moderating the relationship between two others. When considering moderating relationships at level 1, it is important to keep in mind that moderating relationships themselves can be moderated by level 2 predictors. This possibility was discussed in the previous example.

Mediation is said to exist when the relationship between two variables (e.g., x and y) is said to be mediated by a third variable (e.g., z). If x leads to z and then z leads to y, z is said to mediate the relationship between x and y. Evaluating mediation within the multilevel framework is a bit trickier than evaluating moderation, and I will rely heavily on the treatment offered by Bauer, Preacher, and Gil (2006). I cannot cover all the issues they raise, but after reading this volume, their arguments should be more understandable. Nevertheless, I will focus on how Bauer et al. propose to evaluate mediation within level 1 of a two-level model, with the possibility that this mediation is moderated by level 2 differences – so-called moderated mediation.

Bauer et al. suggest an innovative technique to estimate mediation at level 1. They do this by "stacking the data," which means that they repeat the data for an observation and add indicator variables to isolate the mediated relationship and test it. Another use of indicator type variables is presented in Chapter 5 in the section on analyzing simultaneous multiple outcomes. The repeating is not an exact duplicate, but the data are rearranged so that in combination with the indicator variable, the mediated coefficient is estimated.

I will illustrate this technique using data from Tomprou, Nikolaou, and Nezlek (2010). Each day participants provided measures of their positive affect (PA), their perceptions of the promises their employers made to them (ER), and their perceptions of the promises they made to their employers (EE). One of the hypotheses we tested was that employer promises would mediate the significant zero-order relationship between employees' promises and positive affect that we found in our initial analyses.

The raw data for three days of one of our participants for these measures is presented in the top panel of Table 3. The "stacked data" are presented in the bottom panel. To maximize the correspondence between my explanation and Bauer et al.'s, I have included two sets of variable labels, one following the nomenclature offered by Bauer et al., and the other corresponding to the specific variables being analyzed. In these data, ER (employer promises) is the potential mediator (M in Bauer's terms) of the relationship between PA (positive affect, the prime dependent measure, Y in Bauer's terms) and EE (employee promises, a predictor, X in Bauer's terms). The goal of the analyses is to estimate the relationship between a predictor (in this case EE) and a mediator (in this case ER) while simultaneously estimating the relationship between an outcome measure (PA) and the predictor and the mediator. The "trick" to this type of an analysis is the use of indicator variables (dummy-codes) to set up (simultaneously) the equations that are needed to estimate the necessary coefficients.

Table 3   Data File for Mediational Analyses

Day	PA	ER	EE
4	3.67	3.8	3.2
5	1.50	3.8	3.6
6	3.00	2.2	1.6

Bauer terms	Z	Sm	SmX	Sy	SyM	SyX	M	x
Example terms	PA/ER	Ind-M	IM-EE	Ind-Y	IY-ER	IY-EE	ER	EE
	3.67	0.0	0.0	1.0	3.8	3.2	3.8	3.2
	3.8	1.0	3.2	0.0	0.0	0.0	3.8	3.2
	1.5	0.0	0.0	1.0	3.8	3.6	3.8	3.6
	3.8	1.0	3.6	0.0	0.0	0.0	3.8	3.6
	3.0	0.0	0.0	1.0	2.2	1.6	2.2	1.6
	2.2	1.0	1.6	0.0	0.0	0.0	2.2	1.6

The necessary equations are below. These two equations are then combined (see Bauer formula below), and the critical terms are the coefficients for the predictors. Because these are all estimated simultaneously, the coefficient for the predictor in the first equation is the indirect effect between the predictor and the outcome (the mediated relationship), and the coefficient for the predictor in the second equation is the direct effect, adjusted for the indirect effect.

mediator (ER) = intercept + predictor (EE) + error

outcome (PA) = intercept + mediator (ER) + predictor (EE) + error

Following the logic of Bauer et al., the example data include two indicator variables, labeled Ind-M and Ind-Y (Sm and Sy in the Bauer system). The Ind-M indicator (Sm in the Bauer system) is used to estimate coefficients for first equation above, the prediction of the mediator. The Ind-Y indicator (Sy in the Bauer system) is used to estimate coefficients of the second equation, the prediction of the prime dependent measure. Note that there are more variables in the second panel of data than there are in the table presented in Bauer et al. (2006: 146, Figure 3). This is because the table presented by Bauer et al. does not show the critical entries that must be created to conduct the analyses. These additional variables are the products of the indicator variables and the other measures (SmX, SyM, and SyX). For the example study, SmX is labeled as IM-EE (the product of the mediator indicator variable and employee promises), SyM is labeled as IY-ER (the product of the dependent measure indicator variable and employer promises), and SyX is labeled as IY-EE (the product of the dependent measure indicator variable and employee promises).

As will be seen below, the indicator variables set up the estimation of the two equations that are needed to evaluate mediation. Looking at the data in the lower panel, the first line of data models the prediction of PA with an intercept (Sy), the mediator (SyM or ER), and the predictor (SyX or EE). The second line of data models the prediction of ER (the mediator) with an intercept (Sm) and the predictor (SmX or EE). This expansion of one day's data into two entries is then repeated for the next two days.

$$Z_{ij} = d_{Mj}SM_{ij} + a_j(SM_{ij}X_{ij}) + d_{Yj}SY_{ij} + b_j(SY_{ij}M_{ij}) + c_j(SY_{ij}X_{ij}) + eZ_{ij} \, .$$

In this formula, a_j is the indirect effect between the predictor (X) and the outcome, and c_j is the direct effect, controlled for the indirect effect. Here is the model using the nomenclature that has been used in this volume, with the variable names from the specific study taken from Table 3. The sequence of the subscripted βs corresponds to the sequence of the coefficients in the Bauer formula:

$$PA \text{ or } ER_{ij} = \beta_{1j} (\text{Ind-M}) + \beta_{2j} (\text{IM-EE}) + \beta_{3j} (\text{Ind-Y}) + \beta_{4j} (\text{IY-ER}) + \beta_{5j} (\text{IY-EE}) + r_{ij}$$

In the analyses we did, the intercept was dropped, the indicator variables were entered uncentered (because they were dummy codes), and the three measures that were the products of the indicator variables were entered group-mean centered. This analysis produced the following coefficients:

$$y_{ij} = 1.41 \text{ (Ind-M)} + .484 \text{ (IM-EE)} + 4.33 \text{ (Ind-Y)} + .022 \text{ (IY-ER)} + .054 \text{ (IY-EE)} + r_{ij}$$

Interpreting these coefficients is done by estimating predicted values as follows. When Ind-M = 1 and Ind-Y = 0, the last three coefficients are 0 (see the data in the table) because each of these coefficients involves Ind-Y (β_{3j} is Ind-Y, β_{4j} is the product of Ind-Y and ER, and β_{5j} is the product of Ind-Y and EE), so the model reduces to the model below, which is the first three coefficients in the model. Keep in mind that the IM-EE coefficient represents the relationship when EE predicts ER. The IM-EE coefficient was significantly different from 0. So, the indirect relationship between employer promises and PA was significant.

$$y_{ij} = 1.41 \text{ (Ind-M)} + .484 \text{ (IM-EE)} + r_{ij}$$

When Ind-M = 0 and Ind-Y = 1, the model reduces to the model below, and the direct effect of employee promises (.054, the IY-EE term) is not significant. In combination with the significant indirect effect (IM-EE) this means that employer promises fully mediated the relationships between newcomer promises and daily positive affect.

$$y_{ij} = 4.33 \text{ (Ind-Y)} + .022 \text{ (IY-ER)} + .054 \text{ (IY-EE)} + r_{ij}$$

This is pretty heady stuff, and if you do not understand it on the first (or second or third) attempt, don't despair: I had to read and re-read the Bauer et al. article a bunch of times to write this section. Nevertheless, once you understand the logic, it is an informative approach. Bauer et al. also discuss how to examine how such mediational relationships might vary as a function of level 2 differences, but we will have to leave that to the future.

Understanding reliability within the multilevel context

Within classical test or measurement theory, reliability is usually defined in terms of the ratio of true to total variance. For example, in terms of understanding the reliability of a scale or a set of ratings, a coefficient of 1.0 indicates that an instrument measures whatever it measures perfectly, with no error. All the variance in the observed measures is true variance. In contrast, a reliability coefficient of 0 means that none of the observed variance is true variance; the measure is worthless because it measures nothing. For most personality and social psychologists, reliability is usually a concern when a set of measures is intended to measure the same construct. Do different observers see the same behaviors? Do the items that constitute a questionnaire "hang together"? When dealing with multilevel data structures, such questions should be answered with MLM, and I will explain this below.

Before doing this, it is necessary to explain a little about the technical aspects of the algorithms that are at the heart of the programs that are used to conduct MLM. Those of you who are math phobic can relax: there will be no formulas with summation signs and all the letters of the Greek alphabet. And for those of you who are crackerjack statisticians, I beg your indulgence and forgiveness for my sins of omission and commission.

The algorithms that estimate the coefficients in MLM analyses rely on Bayes estimators – more specifically, what is technically referred to as "Bayes shrinkage." In a nutshell, and with all due respect to real statisticians, I offer the following. Take a two-level model. Recall the example I provided in Chapter 2, modified here. Assume we have two classrooms with five students in each. In the first class, the mean score is 5, and the individual students' scores are 1, 1, 5, 9, and 9. In the second class, the mean score is also 5, but the individual students' scores are 4, 5, 5, 5, and 6. The algorithm estimates a set of coefficients for each level 1 unit, in this case, a mean of 5.0 for each class. The algorithm also estimates the reliability of each coefficient for each level 2 unit. Following the example, the mean for the second class is much more reliable than the mean for the first class. The second 5 is "better" than the first 5. Note that OLS analyses such as repeated measures ANOVA do not take such variances into account. In OLS ANOVA, these two 5s would not be distinguished.

When estimating variances, MLM algorithms weight observations by their reliabilities. For purposes of calculating the variances, relatively less reliable observations are "moved" to the mean: hence the "shrinkage" term. The rationale for this is the following. Within a Bayesian framework, the mean (of both intercepts and slopes) is assumed to be valuable in that it provides some information about the population. Broadly speaking, there are two reasons why an observed coefficient is not at the mean of coefficients. First, the coefficient is reliable, and it is in fact a coefficient that (in latent terms) is not at the mean. Second, the coefficient is unreliable, causing the observed coefficient to be further from the mean than it "should be" – i.e., further than the latent (true) coefficient is. Keep in mind that unreliability always leads to inflated estimates of variance compared to the variance of the true scores (observed variance = true variance + error variance).

When calculating the variances, if the coefficient for a unit (e.g., a classroom mean) is less reliable, it is assumed that it would be closer to the mean coefficient if the coefficient was more reliable. And so for some calculations (variances), an observed coefficient is modified, i.e., moved closer to the mean. Moreover, it is the difference between the original "unshrunken" variance estimates and the Bayes-shrunken variance estimates that is part of how MLM programs separate true and random variance. Coefficients that are reliable are not shrunken; they are assumed to be "truly" away from the mean. Note that this procedure does not change estimates of the means of coefficients. The mean is the best unbiased estimator of central tendency, so the mean does not change, but changing variance estimates does change the results of significance tests because significance tests involve comparing a measure of central tendency to a measure of dispersion, and dispersion involves variance.

The truly curious are urged to consult Littell, Milliken, Stroup, and Wolfinger (1996) and Raudenbush and Bryk (2002) which contain detailed explanations of all this. If you are uncomfortable with the idea that the program is changing your data, you can sleep well knowing that estimating coefficients this way produces more accurate estimates than methods that do not involve Bayes shrinkage. Accuracy in this case is defined in terms of how closely the summary statistics provided by a procedure correspond to the known parameters of a population. In Monte Carlo studies, samples are drawn from a population with known parameters and then the estimates of these parameters produced by a technique is compared to the known parameters.

Back to reliability estimates within the program HLM. At first, it may be useful to describe what these reliability estimates are not. For a measure that is the average of a series of items, the reliability of the intercept is not the item level reliability (*à la* Cronbach) of those items. For example, in a diary study, the reliability of the intercept is not the reliability of the scale used in the analysis that produced the intercept. Similarly, when individuals are nested within groups, the reliability of the intercept is not the reliability of items that made up a scale. In both cases, the reliability of the intercept is an indication of the consistency of the responses within level 2 units. How similar are the daily observations for a person, and how similar are the responses of people within each group? The reliability of a slope is an indication of how well a slope represents the relationship between two variables in the groups. Low reliabilities mean that observations within each group do not "cluster around the regression line" that closely, whereas high reliabilities mean that they do.

Most social and personality psychologists are not concerned with such reliabilities, however. They tend to be concerned with the reliability of scales *per se*: how well (how consistently) does a set of items measure a certain construct? This is the question addressed by Cronbach's alpha. To do this properly, items must be nested within another unit of analysis. By adding a level 1 model such as this (sometimes called a measurement model in MLM lingo) the reliability of the level 1 intercept, which as discussed above is a measure of the consistency of the observations within level 2 units, now represents the consistency of responses to a set of items. An example of such a model for a diary style study in which the items for a scale are nested within days which are then nested within persons is as follows:

item level	(level 1)	$y_{ijk} = \pi_{0jk} + e_{ijk}$
day level	(level 2)	$\pi_{0jk} = \beta_{00k} + r_{0jk}$
person level	(level 3)	$\beta_{00k} = \gamma_{000} + \mu_{00k}$

In this model, there are i items nested within j persons nested within k days. The reliability of the level intercept (π) is the item level reliability of the scale, the equivalent of a Cronbach's alpha (which is perfectly appropriate when observations are not nested). If the design was one in which people were nested within groups, the level 1 model would still be a measurement model (i.e., items), but the level 2 model would be people and the level 3 model would be groups. I provide and discuss an example of the application of this technique below. Also see Nezlek and Gable (2001) for an example.

When doing such analyses (regardless of the program being used), it is important that all variables be scored "in the same direction," just as is required in a standard reliability analysis. If some items are administered and are meant to be reverse scored before computing a scale score, those items need to be reversed before estimating the reliability. See the example in Chapter 5, "Using HLM."

Having established what the correct way is to estimate reliability within the multilevel context, I will comment on some bad, wrong, inappropriate, and fundamentally flawed ways to do this (BWIFF). First, within a diary style study, it is BWIFF to calculate within-person means (i.e., aggregated across occasions of measurement) and then calculate a Cronbach's alpha based on these aggregates. This totally confounds between- and within-person variance. To provide an example from a perhaps more easily understood context, I know of few researchers who would aggregate across the observations in a group (when people are nested within groups) and calculate reliabilities on the group level means. If you think that is incorrect, then you should recognize that within the multilevel framework, calculating means within persons when observations are nested within persons is the same as calculating means within groups when people are nested within groups.

Within a diary style study, it is also BWIFF to categorize the data by days and calculate a reliability for each day and then average those reliabilities. This assumes that day 1 for person 1 is matched with day 1 for person 2 and with day 1 for person 3, and so forth. In virtually all instances, this is simply not the case. Days are randomly sampled, and so there is no basis to match any particular day from one person with any particular day from another. Pure babble from the statistical sickbed. Once again for the sake of comparison, in a study in which persons are nested within groups, I know of few researchers who would pick a person from group 1 as person 1, and pick someone from group 2 as person 1, and so forth for all groups, and then calculate reliabilities for person 1, 2 and so forth and average those reliabilities. Most researchers would recognize that this is BWIFF because it is no way to match people, and it just does not make sense to do so. Moreover, what do you do when you have unequal numbers of observations across groups (e.g., unequal numbers of days or unequal numbers of people in groups)? Throw out excess days or people? On what basis? Duplicate days or people to provide equal numbers of observations? Again, on what basis?

Finally, some might argue that you could estimate reliability within each level 2 unit, e.g., within each person in a diary study, or within each group in a group study, and then estimate some type of overall reliability. Conceptually, this is not far from what MLM does (and so it does not qualify for BWIFF status), but technically, it is not as accurate as the estimate provided by MLM.

I think it is easier to understand reliability within the multilevel framework by thinking of reliability as a type of correlation or relationship among items. Just as people use MLM to control for the dependencies and different levels of variance in a set of observations when examining relationships among variables, they need to control for dependencies and variances across different levels when examining reliability. Estimates of reliability that do not do this are simply BWIFF.

Outliers

It may seem a bit odd to follow a section on reliability with one on outliers, but for MLM, the progression is natural. Broadly speaking, outliers undermine the quality of inference because outliers do not "fit in." They lie outside the normal range of the data. As discussed above, via Bayes shrinkage, the algorithms that are standard for multilevel modeling take into account the fact that some observations are far from the mean. So, outliers tend to have less of an influence on the results of MLM than they have on the results of OLS analyses. Nevertheless, Bayes shrinkage is not a cure-all or panacea for bad or weird data. As is the case with any analysis, you should inspect your data for outliers and take appropriate action. This could involve transforming or eliminating observations depending upon the situation.

Modeling causality

For better or worse, causal relationships are implicit in the descriptions of multi-level analyses. Within any particular level of analysis, independent measures are referred to as predictors, and relationships between levels are described similarly. Moreover, for the type of data structures with which social and personality psy-chologists are usually concerned, there is often an assumption that upper level measures have causal precedence over lower level measures. For example, in diary style studies, level 1 observations such as interactions or days of measure-ment are nested within persons, and there is an assumption (however soft an assumption in some quarters) that person level measures such as traits are causes of the types of measures that are collected at the interaction or day level. Similarly, in group studies, group level measures such as leader characteristics are assumed (however softly) to lead to changes in individual level characteristics such as worker performance. Nonetheless, similar to OLS regression, MLM analyses simply esti-mate covariances, relationships between measures, and such estimates do not have any firm, underlying statistical rationale for making inferences about causal relationships.

One way to address issues of causality is to collect measures over time. In our universe, events that occur at time n can be causes of events that occur at time $n + 1$, whereas the reverse causal relationship, from $n + 1$ to n, is presumed to be invalid. So, within the multilevel framework, one can examine causality by collecting data over time and examining relationships between measures collected at time n and those collected at time $n + 1$. Of course, such analyses are limited by the strength of the inference provided by correlational data collected across time, but they can provide support for making causal inferences.

For data structures in which observations are nested within persons and these observations are collected on some regular basis (e.g., every day), it may be possible to do lagged analyses. In such analyses, there are two variables and the goal of the analyses is to determine if the relationship between one variable measured at time $n - 1$ is related to the other at time n, or vice-versa. For example, in Nezlek (2002), I examined lagged relationships between anxiety and self-consciousness. Participants provided data every day, and the following models examined lagged relationships between anxiety and private self-consciousness:

$$\text{PRV(day } n)_{ij} = \beta_{0j} + \beta_{1j}(\text{PRV day } n{-}1) + \beta_{2j}(\text{ANX day } n{-}1) + r_{ij}$$
$$\text{ANX(day } n)_{ij} = \beta_{0j} + \beta_{1j}(\text{PRV day } n{-}1) + \beta_{2j}(\text{ANX day } n{-}1) + r_{ij}$$

The structure of these analyses is similar to that used in OLS regression. Note that in the first model, private self-consciousness on day n is being modeled as a function of anxiety and self-consciousness on the previous day (day $n{-}1$). In the second model, anxiety on day n is also being modeled as a function of anxiety and self-consciousness on the previous day. The critical coefficients are β_{2j} in the first model (actually, the corresponding level 2 coefficient, γ_{20}), and β_{1j} in the second model (γ_{10}). The clearest pattern of results for such analyses is when one lagged coefficient is significant and the other is not (e.g., β_{2j} is significant and β_{1j} is not). Then one can conclude (with some certainty) that one variable causes another, whereas the reverse causal relationship is not viable.

Such analyses are far from perfect statistically speaking. There are lots of factors that need to be considered (e.g., error covariance and the like). Moreover, to my knowledge, there is presently no way within the MLM framework to test differences between coefficients representing lagged relationships when both are significant. I am in the process of developing more sophisticated methods, but I have not worked out the details. Sorry.

Another way to examine causal relationships across time is to examine cross-level relationships. Assume a study of persons nested within groups measured twice (at times T1 and T2). The level 1 (individual level) observations for both time periods are modeled together, as are the level 2 measures. Using a dummy-coded analysis as described above, the T1 and T2 measures can be separated at level 1 with the following model. Note that this model assumes that outcomes are modeled

49

as a function of two dummy-coded variables (T1 and T2 representing time 1 measures and time 2 measures respectively) entered uncentered, with no intercept.

$$y_{ij} = \beta_{1j}(T1) + \beta_{2j}(T2) + r_{ij}$$

In turn, these level 1 means can be modeled at level 2 as a function of variables measured at T1 and T2, which will be referred to as Time1 and Time2.

$$\beta_{1j} = \gamma_{10} + \gamma_{11} \text{ (Time1)} + \gamma_{12} \text{ (Time2)} + \mu_{1j}$$
$$\beta_{2j} = \gamma_{20} + \gamma_{21} \text{ (Time1)} + \gamma_{22} \text{ (Time2)} + \mu_{2j}$$

The lag from the level 1 variable at T1 to the level 2 variable at T2 is tested via the γ_{12} (Time2) coefficient, and the lag from the level 2 variable at T1 to the level 1 variable at T2 is tested via the γ_{21} (Time1) coefficient. Moreover, using the tests of fixed effects, the strength of these lags can be compared (γ_{12} v. γ_{21}).

Non-linear outcomes

So far, I have discussed multilevel analyses in terms of linear (continuous) outcomes. Although my guess is that most readers of this book will be analyzing continuous measures most of the time, there will be times when non-linear outcomes will be of interest. "Non-linear" in this instance refers to categorical responses (e.g., yes/no responses, three or four response options that cannot be scaled) and responses with non-normal distributions (e.g., anything that is heavily skewed). Some readers will be familiar with (or at least will have heard of) logistical regression, and the analysis of non-linear outcomes is multilevel logistical regression.

Building a model to analyze a non-linear outcome is conceptually similar to building a model with linear outcomes. First, the level 1 model is finalized, and then predictors are added at level 2. Similar to linear outcomes, there are significance tests of fixed effects, and interpreting the results is probably best done by estimating predicted values for observations with certain values on variables (±1 SD, different groups, etc.).

As will be immediately apparent when setting up a model (at least in HLM), analyses of non-linear outcomes use different algorithms than analyses of linear outcomes. This will be apparent because the level 1 equation will involve a transformation, and this transformation will vary as a function of the distribution of the dependent measure. This is needed because non-linear measures violate the cardinal rule that means and variances need to be independent. For example, the variance of a binomial distribution is the square root of Npq, where N is the number of observations, p is the probability of the outcome, and q is $1 - p$. Moreover, there will not be an error term at level 1 because the level 1 variance cannot be estimated: the variance varies as a function of the mean.

There are different ways you can interpret the coefficients generated by a non-linear analysis. One is simply to generate predicted values. For categorical data, this is perhaps the simplest when you have a binomial outcome. When you have multiple categories, coefficients represent a function, and this function will have a reference or "home" category. For example, if you have three categories, you will have two coefficients, each of which compares a category to the reference category (e.g., 1 v. 2 and 1 v. 3 or 2 v. 1 and 2 v. 3). With three categories, you cannot have more than two coefficient comparing these categories because this would create linear dependence among the coefficients.

Another popular way of interpreting logistical regressions is to use odds ratios, which are ratios of the odds of events (i.e., responses) occurring. For example, if we had 100 observations and 70 were x and 30 were y, the probability of x would be .7, and the probability of y would be .3. The odds for x would be 2.33 (.7/.3), and the odds for y would be .43 (.3/.7). The odds ratio would then be 5.42 (2.33/.43). The results of an analysis of non-linear outcomes are logits, which can be transformed into odds ratios or probabilities. For those interested in knowing more of the sordid details of all this, I recommend a statistical text that covers logistical regression (e.g., Kleinbaum & Klein, 2002).

Frankly, this stuff can be pretty confusing for those who are not experienced in using and interpreting logistical regression, and I count myself as a member of this group. I will note that when an outcome has three or more categories, I have analyzed (as a fall-back position) a series of binomial variables representing each of the categories in question, e.g., three dummy variables when there are three categories. This is not particularly elegant, and from a statistical point of view it is not the truly proper way to do the analyses. Nevertheless, in my experience, the point estimates from analyses of such binomials are very similar to those derived from the functions mentioned above, and to me, they provide two important advantages. First, I understand exactly what is going on, and I can explain this clearly and unambiguously in a manuscript. Second, I can examine (clearly and unambiguously) relationships between the frequency of occurrence of a category (expressed as a percentage) and a level 2 variable.

For example, assume you are doing a social interaction diary study and you are interested in relationships between personality variables and the percentage of interactions that were same sex only (v. opposite sex only or mixed sex). You could dummy code for same sex (0, 1) at level 1, and then examine relationships between this estimate and the level 2 variables of interest, and you could do the same for opposite sex and mixed sex interactions. Alternatively, you could set a multinomial model (a single variable with three categories) and analyze the data that way. I am not certain that all reviewers and editors will be happy with the simpler procedure (a set of dummy variables), but it can make the results much more accessible. Moreover, if the results of the simpler analyses are functionally equivalent to those of the more complex analyses, this can be mentioned in a footnote to satisfy those who desire complexity.

Unit-specific versus population-average estimates

For non-linear analyses, HLM produces two sets of estimates, a unit-specific estimate and a population-average estimate. (Actually, there are four sets of coefficients, each of these two as robust and non-robust estimates, but the robust distinction, which is explained in the section "Robust parameter estimates" in Chapter 5, applies in the same way to these estimates as it does to estimates for linear outcomes.) Technically, the difference between unit-specific and population-average estimates has something to do with what is called a "link function," an aspect of the analysis that is well beyond the scope of this volume. As a rule of thumb, it probably suffices to say that if you are interested in modeling differences in the overall frequency of occurrence at the population level (e.g., modeling coefficients from an unconditional level 1 model at level 2), then the population-average estimates are probably more appropriate. In contrast, if you are interested in modeling differences across level 1 units, then the unit-specific estimate is probably best. If this explanation has not been sufficiently helpful, a more detailed explanation is provided as part of the help module of the HLM program.

Interpreting results

Regardless of what type of non-linear analysis you perform, I strongly recommend that you use a spreadsheet with built-in transformation algorithms to convert the results of your analyses to odds or probabilities. You can program these transformation routines yourself and simply copy and paste the cells and insert new values when you want to generate point estimates. I recommend doing this because many analysts will be unfamiliar with the types of transformations that are used in non-linear analyses, and it will be difficult to look at the output and have any idea of what the numbers mean.

4

Conceptualizing the Multilevel Structure

When to use MLM

My advice about this is very simple. You should use a multilevel analysis when you have multilevel data. It is neither more nor less complicated than that. Of course, this may be an overly simplistic answer that begs the question: when is a data structure/set multilevel? Perhaps the best way to think of this is to consider the degree of dependence among a set of observations. Can/should units of observation be considered as a group, as having something in common, yet simultaneously differing from one another in other ways? For example, it is fairly obvious that students in individual classes have something in common – their teacher. At the same time, they also differ from each other in terms of their personalities, motives, skills, parents, and so forth. So, we would conceptualize students as nested within classes because measures describing the different students in any specific class are not independent of each other. The students (and therefore the measures describing them) have their teacher, the classroom climate, and so forth in common. Similarly, if we collect diary data (or theoretically, any repeated measure) from an individual, we can, and should in virtually all instances for diary data, conceptualize observations (diary entries) as nested within persons because each diary entry for a person has the person and his/her characteristics in common.

Nevertheless, some researchers recommend using the intraclass correlation (ICC) to determine if a multilevel analysis is appropriate. By the way, the term "intraclass" comes from educational research where it was initially used to describe how much of the variance of a measure was within classes (intra) versus between classes. The ICC represents the ratio of between-group (or level 2 in multilevel terminology) to within-group (level 1) variance. If the ICC is low, it means that groups do not vary very much (relatively speaking). So, the recommendation is that if the ICC is low there is no need to use a multilevel analysis because the groups don't matter – i.e., they do not differ from each other in a meaningful way.

Regardless of the source, such a recommendation, however well intended, is off base for multilevel data structures. As discussed previously, ignoring the

Table 4   Varying within-group relationships when ICCs are 0

Group 1		Group 2		Group 3	
x	y	x	y	x	y
11	5	11	5	11	5
12	4	12	4	12	4
13	3	13	3	13	3
14	2	14	2	14	2
15	1	15	1	15	1
Group 4		Group 5		Group 6	
x	y	x	y	x	y
11	1	11	1	11	1
12	2	12	2	12	2
13	3	13	3	13	3
14	4	14	4	14	4
15	5	15	5	15	5

interdependence (group structure) of a data set can provide inaccurate parameter estimates. My primary concern is that researchers are most often interested in covariances (relationships between variables), and ICCs tell us little or nothing about how relationships between two variables might vary between groups.

For example, in the data presented in Table 4, the ICC for each variable is 0: there is no level 2 variance. For each group, the mean for variable x is 13 and the mean for y is 3. If you analyze all the data as one group, which ignores the grouping structure, the correlation between x and y is 0. If you include a series of dummy codes to represent the groups (the LSDV approach), the x–y correlation is also 0. It is quite clear from the data that in groups 1, 2, and 3 the x–y relationship is negative, whereas in groups 4, 5, and 6 it is positive. So, unless you take the hierarchical structure of these data into account, you get a very misleading answer. Admittedly, the data in this example were contrived to make a point. In practice, such dramatic and clear differences among groups are unlikely. Nevertheless, the possibility that relationships between two variables can vary between units of analysis when the means do not vary, highlights the need to use multilevel analyses even when some would assume otherwise, based on ICCs.

It has been my experience that in the majority of cases determining the nesting or hierarchical structure of a data set is fairly straightforward. For studies of work groups or classrooms, workers or students can be nested within groups or classes respectively. For diary studies, days of observations or interactions can be nested within persons. Similarly, for longitudinal studies, observations across time can be nested within persons.

Nevertheless, there may be times when it is not clear exactly what multilevel structure should be applied to a data set. To me, such possibilities fall into three broad categories. (1) Conceptually, the structure is clear, but there are not enough data to instantiate the conceptual structure. (2) There are plenty of data, but the structure is not clear. (3) The data are such that some level 1 units cannot be unambiguously classified into specific level 2 units. I discuss these in turn.

NB: to nest a set of observations within another set requires at least two "lower level" observations. So, in a diary study, if you have only one day of data for each person, you have no nesting. Both conceptually and technically, you cannot separate days from people. They are confounded (or simply not separable). The absolute minimum number of level 1 observations you need for a level 2 unit is two.

Deciding at what level a variable should be entered

Occasionally, analysts may wonder about the level at which a specific measure should be entered into a model. In most instances, this decision is patently obvious. In a two-level structure in which students are nested within classrooms, student level measures (grades, study time, etc.) would be included at level 1, and classroom level measures (size, teacher experience, etc.) would be included at level 2. Similarly, in a two-level structure in which days are nested within persons, day level measures (e.g., different types of events) would be included at level 1, and personal level measures (e.g., personality) would be included at level 2. And so forth.

There is a situation, however, in which what would seem to be a level 1 characteristic/measure is included in a model at level 2. When there is no variability within level 2 units for a level 1 measure, that level 1 measure needs to be represented (entered) in the model at level 2. For example, if I have a study of students nested within classrooms, and all the classrooms are same sex, the student level (level 1) variable of sex has become a level 2 measure. I would include sex (in whatever fashion made sense) at level 2. There is no within-unit variability on sex, and so it makes no sense to conceptualize the measure at level 1. In this instance, sex has become a classroom level characteristic, similar to class size or the subject of the class (e.g., language v. science).

Creating level 2 measures from some type of aggregation of a level 1 measure is entirely appropriate, as long as one keeps in mind what the measures and the cross-level relationships represent. For example, in a classroom study, one could create a variable representing the percentage of boys in a classroom and examine relationships between this percentage and the academic achievement of boys and girls, or the sex difference in achievement.

Clear structure, not enough data

There may be times when an analyst has a certain multilevel structure in mind, but there are simply not enough data to use this structure as an analytic framework, and I discuss such a possibility using an example from my own research.

The study concerned cross-cultural similarities and differences in relationships between daily events and self-evaluation and affect. Participants in Japan, Canada, and two culturally different sites in the US (one was Hampton University, a historically black college, the other was William & Mary) maintained a daily diary for about two weeks. In each of the four sites, there were between 80 and 100 participants. There were plenty of days for each person and plenty of people at each site. See Nezlek, Sorrentino et al. (2008) for details about the samples.

When the study was designed and the data were collected, the study was conceptualized as a three-level structure in which days were nested within persons which were nested within cultures. Initially, three-level models were run first (as per the original design), but it was clear that the three-level models exceeded the "carrying capacity" of the data. There were simply not enough data to estimate the parameters required by a three-level model. As it turned out, there were not enough countries represented by the level 2 units (people) to nest persons within a third (upper) level. Various types of two-level models were also run, and the analyses presented below represent the best solutions to analyze the data at hand.

The primary hypotheses concerned cultural differences in reactions to events, i.e., within-person relationships between events and various outcomes such as self-esteem. Within multilevel terms, the hypotheses concerned slopes between events and outcome measures. In the published article, we distinguished four types of events, combinations of positive–negative and social–achievement, and we examined six outcomes. In the interests of parsimony, I will discuss modeling options using only two events (positive v. negative) and one outcome, self-esteem.

At first glance, the data obviously required a three-level model: days nested within persons, and persons nested within cultures. The equations for such a model are below. There are i days nested within j persons nested within k cultures. Positive and negative events were entered at level 1 group-mean centered.

level 1 (day) $y_{ijk} = \pi_{0jk} + \pi_{1jk} (\text{Positive}) + \pi_{2jk} (\text{Negative}) + e_{ijk}$

level 2 (person) $\pi_{0jk} = \beta_{00k} + r_{0jk}$

                      $\pi_{1jk} = \beta_{10k} + r_{1jk}$

                      $\pi_{2jk} = \beta_{20k} + r_{2jk}$

level 3 (culture) $\beta_{00k} = \gamma_{000} + \mu_{00k}$

                      $\beta_{10k} = \gamma_{100} + \mu_{10k}$

                      $\beta_{20k} = \gamma_{200} + \mu_{20k}$

Initially, the model was successful. It converged in a reasonable number of iterations (300 or so, a little high, but not bad), and it was possible to estimate all the random error terms. Nevertheless, it was not possible to test the hypotheses of the study, which involved differences at level 3. When comparisons among the four sites were done with anything other than a single dummy code, the model broke down: various important parameters could not be estimated. The reason for this was that although there were enough cultures (sites) to estimate the level 3 random error terms *per se*, there were not enough sites to model the level 3 variance – the differences among cultures. Such a situation raises questions about how many units of analysis are needed to constitute a level, a topic discussed below.

The solution to this problem was to "move" culture down to the person level. Site became an individual difference variable. This was done with a series of dummy codes. As suggested in Chapter 2 in the section on using categorical predictors, each site was represented by a dummy code, all four dummy codes were entered simultaneously, and the intercept was dropped at level 2 (the person level, now the top level in a two-level model). These analyses produced separate estimates (coefficients) for each of the four sites (WM, HU, UWO, JP) – estimates that could then be compared using the tests of fixed effects described earlier. This model was very stable, and it allowed for comparisons involving any combination of sites. The final model we used is as follows:

$$\begin{aligned} \text{level 1 (day)} \quad & y_{ij} = \beta_{0j} + \beta_{1j}\,(\text{Positive}) + \beta_{2j}\,(\text{Negative}) + r_{ij} \\ \text{level 2 (person)} \quad & \beta_{0j} = \gamma_{01}\,(\text{WM}) + \gamma_{02}\,(\text{HU}) + \gamma_{03}\,(\text{UWO}) + \gamma_{04}\,(\text{JP}) + \mu_{0j} \\ & \beta_{1j} = \gamma_{11}\,(\text{WM}) + \gamma_{12}\,(\text{HU}) + \gamma_{13}\,(\text{UWO}) + \gamma_{14}\,(\text{JP}) + \mu_{1j} \\ & \beta_{2j} = \gamma_{21}\,(\text{WM}) + \gamma_{22}\,(\text{HU}) + \gamma_{23}\,(\text{UWO}) + \gamma_{24}\,(\text{JP}) + \mu_{2j} \end{aligned}$$

In this example, the desired structure was clear, but the data were not sufficient to estimate the parameters entailed by a three-level model. In contrast, there may be times when it is not clear how many or what levels an analysis should contain. Broadly speaking, there are two types of such situations. First, should an analysis take account of a certain level or type of nesting, and second, what should be nested within what?

Structure not clear

To nest or not to nest? That is the question. The answer lies not in our stars, but in the importance of controlling for possible confounding variances across possible levels of analysis. Imagine a diary study in which observations (e.g., an emotional state and a measure of the situation) are collected multiple times each day across multiple days – a "beeper" study. The question is, do you run a three-level model in which observations are nested within days that are nested within persons, or a two-level model in which observations are nested within persons? The first issue to consider is how many days are available, how different days might be, and how important differences between days are. If the answers are not many, not much, and not at all, then a two-level model (observations nested within persons) may suffice.

For a study such as this, regardless of the assumed strength and importance of differences across days, it is probably best to add the day as a level of nesting when practical. This will control for whatever variance exists at the day level. Just as it is possible for a between-group effect to masquerade as an individual level effect when the grouped structure of a "person within group" data set is ignored, it is possible for a day level effect to masquerade as a between-person effect.

It is entirely possible for two measures to be negatively related (or unrelated) at the within-day (occasion of measurement) level while being positively related at the between-day level. If the day level variation is ignored, then analyses will confound day and occasion level relationships, and possibly lead to an incorrect estimate of the occasion level relationship. Such a possibility is illustrated by the data presented in Table 5. Note that such problems are not conceptually different than the general issue of separating variances at different levels of analysis – the basic goal of MLM.

Table 5   Confounding of occasion and day level relationships

		Depression	Anxiety
Day 1	Occ 1	9	7
	Occ 2	8	8
	Occ 3	7	9
	Occ 4	9	7
	Occ 5	8	8
	Occ 6	7	9
Day 2	Occ 1	6	4
	Occ 2	5	5
	Occ 3	4	6
	Occ 4	6	4
	Occ 5	5	5
	Occ 6	4	6
Day 3	Occ 1	3	1
	Occ 2	2	2
	Occ 3	1	3
	Occ 4	3	1
	Occ 5	2	2
	Occ 6	1	3

Structure clear, data ambiguous

There are times when the structure of a data set is quite clear, but the data do not cleanly or unambiguously fall into that structure. One such instance of this is called multiple membership in the MLM lexicon. This occurs when a level 1 unit changes the level 2 unit under which it nested (or within which it is clustered). For example, in a study of group process, an individual changes groups. When the data are analyzed, to which group should the individual be assigned, the original or the final?

Unfortunately (for present purposes), the program HLM does not have a built-in procedure for analyzing such data; however, such analyses can be done using the program MLwiN, and this procedure is explained in the MLwiN manual (Rabash, Steele, Browne, & Goldstein, 2009: 283–286) and in the help system of the MLwinN program. Explaining these procedures in detail would require explaining how to use MLwiN, which is a bit beyond what I can and want to do here. Nevertheless, in brief, the procedure involves setting up a series of weighted indicator variables (one for each group) that represent the proportion of time an individual has spent in each group. These weights are then used in the model to weight observations.

The second type of ambiguity occurs when the upper level units in which level 1 units are nested overlap or are not clear, a situation that is called cross-classification in the MLM lexicon. The classic example of this is in studies of children who are nested within schools, but some schools have students from different neighborhoods. So, when trying to disentangle the effects of schools and neighborhoods, this lack of clear nesting needs to be taken into account. The solution is to set up a matrix that represents the various combinations of schools and neighborhoods. In the HLM program, this is done by using a special MDM file created by selecting the HCM option. Once again, this is an advanced topic that I cannot cover here. How to do this is explained in the manuals that accompany software packages.

Data management

In this section I address some practical, "nuts and bolts" issues concerning how to incorporate the multilevel perspective into how you conceptualize and organize your data. On the more practical side, when thinking of data preparation and organization for multilevel analysis, it is important to keep the "multi" part of multilevel in mind. How you manage your data should reflect how you conceptualize your data. Moreover, for a multilevel data structure, the issues inherent in managing the data for any project are multiplied by the fact that for a multilevel data structure, data at different levels of analysis and their combination need to be managed simultaneously. I urge analysts to anticipate this complexity and create some type of organizing structure before beginning analyses. Creating such a structure will help organize one's thinking and will make it easier to organize the various analyses that will be produced. It will also minimize the inefficiency inherent in going through a lengthy list of output files and classifying them after the fact.

Along these lines, I think it is important from the outset to separate clearly the data for each level of analysis. In terms of the details of using a computer, for each project for which the data will be analyzed using a two-level model, I typically have at least three "folders" or "directories" (or whatever organizing unit you want to call them). I place the raw data and all the accompanying transformation programs (e.g., syntax or command files) and output files from these programs for the level 1 data in one folder, and the corresponding files for the level 2 data in another folder. I place the results of the actual multilevel analyses in a third folder, with subfolders for different types of analyses.

Such separation highlights which constructs are being measured at which levels of analysis. The program HLM (to be discussed below) requires that the data for different levels of analysis are contained in different files. The program then joins these files to create a system file that is used to conduct analyses. In some other programs, users must join files from different levels of analysis themselves, attach trait level measures to the corresponding daily measures for a person, attach teacher level data to the data for each child in a classroom, and so forth. Nevertheless, even when using a program in which the data from different levels of analysis need to be joined by the user, I still recommend keeping the data separate. Certainly, individual users can decide what is best for them. I just happen to find that the explicit separation of the data for each level of analysis helps to simplify and clarify what can be a very complicated data structure (or mess).

Standardization

As discussed previously, multilevel analysis programs provide only unstandardized coefficients, begging questions about standardization. In this section, I discuss the implications of standardization at different levels of analysis to provide a basis to allow individual analysts to make decisions about standardizing their own data.

For a two-level model, standardizing at level 2 is probably the most straightforward decision (as it is for level 3 in a three-level model). Standardizing measures at level 2 has no effect on the significance tests of individual coefficients – they are invariant under transformation; however, standardization can affect the results of tests that compare coefficients (see section "Comparing coefficients" in Chapter 2). Such tests are not invariant under transformation (a characteristic that riles some purists). Putting this aside, standardizing at level 2 makes it easier to interpret coefficients because when level 2 measures are standardized, a 1 unit change in a coefficient corresponds to a 1 SD change. This is particularly useful given that regression analyses are often interpreted in terms of estimated values ±1SD. Whenever level 2 units are people (e.g., participants in a diary study in which observations are nested within persons; teachers or supervisors in which students or workers are nested, etc.), I usually standardize person level measures such as personality traits.

Standardizing at level 1 in a two- or three-level model (or at level 2 in a three-level model) is not quite as straightforward. The preferred method of standardization is to standardize based on the grand mean, i.e., standardize the data without regard to the group or nested structure. Similar to standardizing measures at level 2, standardizing measures this way has no effect on the significance tests of individual coefficients – they are invariant under transformation; however, standardization can affect the results of tests that compare coefficients. Unlike the standardization of measures at level 2, standardizing level 1 data in this way does not provide the basis for straightforwardly estimating coefficients ± 1 SD from a mean. As noted previously in the section "Interactions" in Chapter 3, standard deviations at level 1 (and at level 2 in a three-level model) should be estimated by taking the square root of the variance of a measure at the appropriate level of analysis from an unconditional model of the measure. Standardizing a measure will change such variance estimates, leading to a change in the estimate of the level 1 (within-unit) standard deviation.

I do not recommend standardizing at level 1 in a two- or three-level model (or at level 2 in a three-level model) by standardizing within units of analysis. For example, in a diary study this would occur if level 1 data (e.g., diary entries) were standardized within each person, or in a classroom or work group study if level 1 data (students or workers) were standardized within each classroom or work group. Such procedures remove from a model the between-unit variance in a measure – the mean for all units of analysis becomes 0 – and such variation is an important part of the model. One could add some number to the standardized values for each unit (perhaps the original mean for a unit of analysis), but then one would be faced with a standard within-unit variance of 1 and a between-unit variance of whatever was generated by such additions.

Regardless, analysts should be mindful of the implications that standardizing their data will have for the results of their analyses. In particular, they should keep in mind that standardizing level 1 data around the grand mean (as recommended above) is a *de facto* method of grand-mean centering. That is, if a level 1 predictor that has been standardized around the grand mean is entered into an analysis uncentered, the resulting coefficients need to be interpreted as if the predictors had been grand-mean centered. Recall that when a predictor is entered uncentered, the intercept represents the expected value for an observation that has a value of 0 on the predictor. When a predictor is standardized around the grand mean, the grand mean becomes 0: hence the equivalence of grand-mean centering and no centering for variables standardized around the grand mean.

Missing data

When discussing missing data within the multilevel framework, it is important to distinguish missing data from missing observations. Missing data are measures that were intended to be taken but were not. For example, in a daily diary study that occurred over two weeks in which days are nested within participants, if a participant did not record how many stressors occurred during a specific day, that would be a missing datum at level 1. If a participant did not complete a personality measure, that would be a missing datum at level 2. If a participant did not record all of the data for an entire day – he or she just skipped a day – those data would not be treated as missing. Rather, that participant would have fewer days (13 level 1 observations) than participants who provided data each day (14 level 1 observations).

When setting up the data files for a diary study such as this, there is no reason to have the same number of days for each person and to enter blanks for all of the measures for days that someone did not maintain the diary. Another way to think of this issue is to recognize the similarity between the multilevel analyses needed for such a study and the analyses needed for a study in which students are nested within classrooms or one in which interactions are nested within persons. There is no requirement that different classrooms have the same number of students, just as there is no requirement that people have the same number of interactions.

Within the multilevel framework, missing data are handled in a straightforward fashion, albeit with some differences across programs (I discuss how HLM handles missing data in Chapter 5, "Using HLM"). Missing data are allowed at level 1, but are not allowed at other levels (level 2 in a two-level structure, and levels 2 and 3 in a three-level structure). Full stop. So, in a two-level data structure such as persons nested within work groups, missing data are allowed at the worker level but not at the group level. If daily observations are nested within persons, missing data are allowed at the daily level, but not at the person level. In a three-level data structure such as occasions nested within days and days nested within persons (the type of data produced by many "beeper" studies), missing data are allowed at the occasion (beeped) level, but not at the day or person level.

Regardless of the program, if a case at an upper level of analysis has a missing value on a variable that is included in an analysis, that case and all the cases that are nested underneath it are excluded. So, in a diary study, if a person is missing a trait level (person level) measure, that person and all his or her diary entries are excluded from analyses that include that trait level measure.

The preceding discussion has not considered instances in which data might be missing systematically. For example, in a social interaction diary study, individuals might be asked to indicate if a romantic partner was present in each interaction, and using the coding techniques described above, interactions could be classified as a function of whether a romantic partner was present or not. In my social interaction diary studies of collegians, typically about half (or a little more) record at least one interaction with a romantic partner during the course of the typical two- to three-week study. For example, in the study described in Nezlek and Smith (2005), 62 of the 130 participants recorded at least one interaction with a romantic partner.

The question at hand is, how should the lack of interactions involving a romantic partner be treated? In some sense, these are missing data. Should participants who had no interactions with a romantic partner contribute to analyses that compare the two types of interactions? The following example illustrates the effect that including and excluding people (level 2 units in this case) who are systematically missing a type of interaction (level 1 unit) has on parameter estimates involving the type of interaction that many are missing.

One way of examining this issue is to compare interactions that involved and did not involve a romantic partner using a dummy-coded variable (as discussed above) for which interactions involving a romantic partner are coded 1 and those that did not are coded 0. An analysis of the full sample ($n = 130$) of how intimate participants felt their interactions were estimated a "romantic effect" of 2.106, with an intercept of 4.988. The dummy variable was entered uncentered, which meant that the intercept represented the mean intimacy when a romantic partner was not present. A similar analysis of the sample that was limited to participants who had at least one interaction with a romantic partner ($n = 62$) estimated the "romantic effect" to be 2.016, with an intercept of 5.143. The standard errors of the fixed effects for the two "romantic effects" were .182 and .199 respectively.

These analyses suggest that including or excluding level 2 units that are systematically missing a type of level 1 observation may change estimates of level 1 coefficients involving that type of level 1 observation. Such a possibility is also suggested by the inclusion of level 2 variables as predictors. In the study cited above, we also collected measures of neuroticism. When neuroticism was included as a level 2 predictor of the romantic effect, although the coefficients from the two samples describing the relationships between neuroticism and the romantic effect were not significant, they were not the same: full sample, −.093 (SE = .152); partial sample, .013 (SE = .165).

Although the substantive conclusions in this example did not differ sharply, it is impossible to predict the effect on results of including or excluding cases that have systematically missing data. Moreover, aside from statistical issues of estimation, if cases are systematically missing certain types of observations (e.g., romantic partner, cross-racial interactions, etc.), there may be issues of generalizability. Is it appropriate to use people who have no contact with members of ethnic groups other than their own to estimate differences between inter- and intra-ethnic contact? Such questions are not about data analyses *per se*; they concern sampling and the design of studies.

Alternatives to MLM for multilevel data

Having made a strong case for using multilevel modeling when you have multilevel data, I allow that there may be times when you should not or cannot use multilevel modeling when you have multilevel data. One of the features of a multilevel data structure is that units of analysis have been sampled from multiple populations simultaneously, e.g., classes and schools. Correspondingly, the analyses have two targets of inference: the population from which the level 2 units were drawn (e.g., classes) and the population from which the level 1 units were drawn (e.g., students).

When thinking of a multilevel analysis, the fact that inferences are being made to populations on the basis of samples provides a context for determining if a multilevel model is appropriate: are there enough observations to provide a basis for making an inference? Sometimes, the answer to this question will be "No." For example, in a cross-cultural study, if people are nested within countries, and there are only three countries, then there are not enough countries to draw an inference about countries *per se*. This, of course, begs two questions: how many are enough, and what do you do if you do not have enough? The first question is discussed in the section "Power: sample sizes," and I address the second question here.

If you have a multilevel data set but do not have enough level 2 units to provide a basis for inference (a lack of level 2 units is by far the more common problem), there are good alternatives. Assume you have collected data from France, Germany, and the UK with numerous respondents in each country. Within the context of OLS regression (with the respondent as the unit of analysis), you can enter terms representing the different countries and terms representing how relationships between a predictor and a dependent measure vary across countries (i.e., the interaction). You can also run a "regression by groups" analysis. Such an analysis produces a test of the similarity of the regression equations across groups (three countries in the present example), and provides a context within which slopes for different countries can be compared.

Although such analyses are multilevel and allow for the possibility that slopes vary across units of analysis, they are limited in some ways. The substantive limitation is that it is not possible to model statistically differences across the groups (the level 2 units). Continuing the country example, we might know that the slope for a certain predictor differs between France and Germany, but we cannot explain (statistically) why this difference exists. There are not enough countries to provide a basis for making inferences about the association between country level characteristics and the within-country relationships estimated by the regression analysis. In closing, I will note that I have read reviews (not necessarily of my own manuscripts) in which well-intentioned (but poorly informed) reviewers have insisted that a data set be analyzed using MLM when there were clearly not enough observations to justify such analyses.

Power: sample sizes

When writing about MLM, power is the topic that makes me the most uncomfortable because, despite some decent scholarly attention, it is still not well understood.

The difficulty in estimating the power of different designs reflects the complexity of the parameters that are typically estimated with an MLM. Consider a simple model in which a level 1 mean (intercept from an unconditional model) is brought up to level 2. The ability to detect relationships between these intercepts and level 2 variables will be a function of the number of level 2 observations and the strength of the relationships between the level 2 measures and the level 1 intercepts (just like in OLS – more and stronger is easier than fewer and weaker) and the reliability of the level 1 intercepts (not a factor in OLS – and more reliable is easier).

For slopes *per se*, power will depend upon the size of the fixed part of the coefficient (how big the relationship is), how reliable it is, with the important caveat that reliability cannot be calculated when a random error term is not estimated, and the number of level 1 and level 2 observations. The power to detect moderation of these slopes by level 2 variables will depend upon the ease with which the level 1 coefficients can be estimated, and the number of level 2 observations and the strength of the moderating relationships.

When thinking about power within MLM, the trade-off between the number of level 1 and level 2 units needs to be considered. If you have a weak level 1 relationship you might be able to "catch it" (model it) if you have lots of level 2 observations. To an extent, increasing the number of level 2 observations can offset the unreliability of a level 1 slope.

I wish that I could provide a better basis for making recommendations. As you may have inferred from this text, I am not shy about recommending *per se*. I am simply not all that confident about the recommendations that have been offered to date. In my own work (diary study), I typically run a study for two weeks with about 100–150 participants, and this seems to work for me. In a social interaction diary study, I will have about 30–50 interactions nested within 50–100 participants. Again, these types of numbers have served me well.

For more formal (and perhaps more informative) discussions of power within the multilevel framework, I recommend Maas and Hox (2005), a section in Richter (2006), and Scherbaum and Ferreter (2009). There are various rules of thumb that are discussed in each of these.

Reporting guidelines

I describe below what I consider to be the critical features of MLM that should be described in research reports (journal articles, chapters, etc.), and I respectfully suggest that these specific guidelines be considered within the following, more general context. First, unless you are writing for *Psychological Methods* or something like that, the statistics and the analyses themselves should be less important than the substantive findings. Occasionally, you may need or want to describe aspects of your analyses in detail, but for the most part, the analyses are a means to an end, not an end in and of themselves. Second, unless you explicitly know otherwise, assume that your readers will vary considerably in terms of their understanding of MLM. My sense is that many social and personality psychologists will never become familiar with the nuances of MLM because they will not have to know MLM for their own work. Regardless, they may be interested in your substantive conclusions.

Overall, when describing the results of MLM analyses, there is often a tension between saying too much (and the analyses themselves become the focus, your readers' eyes start rolling, and no one cares what you have done) and saying too little (and no one knows what you have done and pays no attention for that reason). The balance between these two will vary from article to article and journal to journal, and it will probably change across time. Nonetheless, I think you should keep this balance in mind as you prepare manuscripts. Finally, when thinking of reporting details, I recommend providing enough detail so that a reader could repeat your analyses if he or she wanted to.

Some necessities

The data structure.   Readers need to be told in clear terms what was nested within what. Do not assume that they will figure it out or that it is obvious. Such descriptions should include the number of observations at each level of analysis: e.g., in a diary study, how many people and how many days or interactions; in a group study, how many groups and how many people; and so forth. Moreover, for lower levels of analysis (e.g., level 1 in a two-level model) the distribution of the number of level 1 observations should be described, e.g., the mean and SD of the number of level 1 observations for level 2 units. It may be helpful in some circumstances to provide minima and maxima, or the percentage of level 2 units that had a certain number of level 1 observations.

Centering.   How each variable at each level of analysis was centered should be described explicitly. This can be done simply by saying something such as, "All continuous level 1 predictors were entered group-mean centered." If you have a rationale for why you chose a certain centering option over others, provide it. The results of your analyses cannot be understood without knowing how predictors were centered. If predictors were entered uncentered, say so. Not centered is a type of centering. Moreover, as we have discussed, results can change as a function of centering. Take special note of the fact that when level 1 predictors are standardized around the grand mean (which is perfectly appropriate) and entered uncentered, they are in fact being entered grand-mean centered.

Model equations.   Given the complexity of some MLM analyses and the present lack of familiarity among many readers with MLM, I recommend presenting the equations representing the models that were run. This may change if more people become more familiar with MLM, but for now, I think it best to do so. Also, *à la* Bryk and Raudenbush and how I have described models here, I strongly recommend presenting the model equations for each level of an analysis separately. I think this makes clear what was done, particularly for readers who are not familiar with MLM. It may not be necessary to describe each and every model, but the basic structure should be presented. For example, if you are running a series of analyses that have the same level 1 predictors but you are varying the level 2 predictors, you could provide the model equations and describe the fact that numerous level 2 predictors will be used. By the way, this recommendation does not mean that I think modelers need to use HLM; rather, I think that the way in which Bryk and Raudenbush present models is more easily understood than the primary alternative – one (sometimes long) equation with all predictors from all levels put together. For those of you who believe that "Well, readers should educate themselves about what MLM is so they can understand the real equations," I encourage you to be more sympathetic to readers who are less knowledgeable. Most articles written by social and personality psychologists are not about modeling, they are about substantive conclusions.

Modeling of random error. With few exceptions, the types of coefficients with which social and personality psychologists are concerned should be modeled as random, and how random error terms were modeled should be described explicitly. This does not need to include a description of each and every error term, but the decision rules that were used to fix effects should be described explicitly. Moreover, if coefficients are treated as fixed on some basis other than statistical tests, the reason for this should be explained. Nonetheless, in most cases it is not necessary to discuss error structures in detail. Few hypotheses explicitly concern error structures *per se*, and extended discussions of error terms may distract readers more than they clarify the results of a study.

Descriptive statistics. The basic descriptive statistics for a multilevel data structure, means and variance estimates for each level, are provided by unconditional analyses. Providing such descriptive statistics for dependent and independent measures in an article provides a context that can help readers understand your results.

Some recommendations

Reporting results of statistical tests. I encourage authors to be sparing in terms of the details of their statistical tests they report. For example, most hypotheses are tested by some type of gamma (level 2) coefficients, which are tested for significance with an approximate t-ratio. These t-ratios are the quotients of estimates of fixed effects (gamma) divided by corresponding standard errors. Given this, there is no need to present the gamma, the t-ratio, and the standard error. Any two will do because the third can be derived from the other two. To me, it makes the most sense to present the gamma and the t-ratio for an effect, with the associated p-value. Too often, I review articles in which all sorts of excess, extraneous, and essentially uninformative statistics are presented – at times, I suspect, because the authors are not certain what is important, so they present anything and everything. See next point.

Descriptions of model fits and comparisons of sequential models. Unlike SEM (structural equation modeling) in which goodness of fit tests are the *sine qua non* of a model, the focus of most MLM analyses is the fixed effect part of coefficients that test relationships. Fit indices include both the fixed and random components, and unless hypotheses concern error structures *per se*, overall model fits may be testing differences between models that are not of concern. Along these lines, sequential comparisons of models typically offer few insights above and beyond what are provided by final models. If the changes in a model that occur as a result of the sequencing of predictors make a substantive contribution then by all means, the sequences should be reported. On the other hand, if sequential tests are reported primarily to provide some type of statistical justification for a final model, reporting the details of sequential tests may confuse more than it clarifies.

Illustrating results with predicted values. I think presenting predicted values can be a very useful way of describing results, particularly when the results concern complicated interactions. Returning to the cross-level moderation of a within-person interaction I described previously, I cannot imagine how an individual could understand the pattern of results of this analysis from the coefficients themselves. When there are groups, it helps readers understand the nature of the differences between groups when they read that the coefficients for group 1 were such-and-such, whereas the coefficients for group 2 were this-and-that.

Graphs. For written presentations (articles, chapters, etc.) I am not a big fan of graphs. They take up a lot of space, and by manipulating the axes, you can enhance or diminish relationships. Noting this, some people are fans of graphs, and if you think your audience cannot understand that a slope of .75 means that a change in one variable is associated with a bigger change in another variable compared to a slope of .10, then I guess you should use graphs. For presentations, when you are competing with God-knows-what for the attention of your audience, graphs might make more sense if only because your audience will have some figures to look at instead of just numbers.

Software options

The increase in popularity of MLM has been accompanied by (or has led to, or is the result of) an increase in the availability of programs that conduct multilevel analyses. Broadly speaking, there are two types of such programs: those intended to do only (or primarily) multilevel analyses (e.g., HLM and MLwiN), and general purpose programs that can do multilevel analyses (e.g., SAS). This is not the forum to provide a systematic review of all the available options; however, I will provide some broad guidance.

Particularly for less experienced modelers, my general recommendation is to use a special purpose program. I use and specifically recommend the program HLM, but this recommendation for a specific program reflects a more general concern. I recommend using a special purpose program because I think it is easier to set up models and to interpret the results using a special purpose program than it is using a general purpose program. With special purpose programs, the interfaces and output formats are designed specifically for multilevel modeling. This means that modeling options that are commonly used within a multilevel context and the specific summary statistics and results of interest to a multilevel modeler are more readily accessible than they might be within a general purpose program.

When using general purpose programs, I have often seen (with both experienced and inexperienced modelers) analysts specify models that they did not intend to test, without recognizing that they were not actually testing the model they wanted to test. Similarly, I have seen analysts (more so with inexperienced than with experienced modelers) pore over the results of a multilevel analysis searching for the summary statistics that would let them know if their model "worked." Moreover, I have seen analysts use the wrong statistics from the results produced by general purpose programs to test their hypotheses.

Nevertheless, when properly set up and interpreted, general purpose programs can do exactly the same analyses as specialized programs and can provide exactly the same summary statistics that can be used to test hypotheses. Moreover, general purpose programs can perform specialized analyses that special purpose programs cannot. For example, SAS can be used to examine the possibility that units of analysis can be clustered based on error covariance structures, whereas HLM cannot do anything like this. As an analyst and the questions he or she asks become more sophisticated, it may very well be that the additional capabilities of a general purpose program become desirable or even necessary. For example, HLM is limited to two- or three-level models, and although I think two- and three-level models are all that is needed for most applications, an analyst may legitimately need a model with more than three levels.

My summary recommendation to use HLM is based on my experience using the program and giving workshops. The program is very accessible. The interface is easy to use, and the results are thorough without being cumbersome. Moreover, there is sufficient flexibility ("bells and whistles") to provide the ability to test fairly sophisticated hypotheses. I will note that I do not receive (nor have I ever received) any compensation of any kind from Scientific Software International for using or recommending the HLM program. I use and recommend it because I like using it, and because I have had success teaching people how to do multilevel analyses using HLM.

By the way, you can download a free (with no expiration date) version of HLM at http://ssicentral.com/hlm/student.html. This free version is fully functional, although it does limit the number of predictors and the number of observations in analyses. Noting these limitations, I could have used the free version to do the analyses for the vast majority (perhaps 90%) of the papers I have published that have used multilevel modeling.

5

Using HLM

Although it may seem a bit out of place to describe how to use a specific program in a book such as this, one of my goals in writing this book was to provide people with the knowledge they would need to do multilevel analyses, and given the specialized nature of the software needed for MLM, some type of description of a software application was called for. Nevertheless, I do not provide a thorough explanation that covers all aspects and options because the help section of the program, which also comes with the free version of the program mentioned at the end of the previous chapter, is very thorough. I do, however, provide enough detail to get readers started. Moreover, once I begin to discuss how to do analyses *per se*, although I will use the HLM program to illustrate certain points, the recommendations and aspects of modeling I mention are not specific or limited to the HLM program.

The logic of the program is as follows. Raw data are used to create what is called a MDM (multilevel data matrix) file. This is similar to a SAV file in SPSS or a SAS file in SAS, and this file is used as the basis for analyses. In earlier versions of HLM, such a file was called a SSM file. When a MDM file is created, two other files are automatically created. One is a ".sts" file that is always named "HLM2MDM.STS" for a two-level file or "HLM3MDM.STS" for a three-level file. It contains simple summary statistics (number of valid observations, mean, maximum, minimum, and standard deviation) of the variables at each level of analysis. I strongly recommend renaming and saving STS files for future reference. The file should be renamed because HLM sometimes will overwrite files without asking before doing so, and once a file is overwritten it is lost. Moreover, it is particularly helpful to rename the STS file so that it corresponds to the name for the MDM file.

It is important to note that in a STS file, the standard deviations for measures at lower levels of analysis (level 1 in two- and three-level models, and level 2 in a three-model) do not reflect the nested structure of the data. They are based on a "flat file". As noted elsewhere, for lower levels of analysis, within-unit standard deviations need to be estimated from variance estimates produced by unconditional models of variables. STS files are simple text files that can be opened with a program such as Notepad in a Windows operating system.

When a MDM file is created, a MDMT file is also created (MDM template). In earlier versions of HLM, such a file was called a RSP file. This file contains the commands used to create the MDM file: the names of the data files for each level of analysis, the names of the variables selected, missing value description, and so forth. MDMT files are simple text files. I recommend naming the MDMT file with the same prefix as used to name the MDM file. In combination with a renamed STS file, this would provide three files for each database: the MDM file itself, the MDMT file that was used to generate it, and the STS file that contains a snapshot summary of the data in the MDM file. In addition, MDMT files can be read into HLM to regenerate a MDM file and can be modified to create a new MDM file. This last feature can be very helpful when one wants to add variables or cases to an existing MDM file.

Models are built by selecting variables that are in the MDM file. A variable is selected as a dependent measure (called an outcome), and then predictors are added as desired. Following the logic introduced by Bryk and Raudenbush, the equations for each level of the model are presented separately. The commands that generate an analysis can be saved as a HLM file. A specific analysis always produces a summary of the results (an example of which is discussed below), which is a simple text file, and analyses can also produce graphs and residual files, which are discussed briefly below.

I will be using sample data sets as a basis for discussing how to use HLM. These data sets and various files are available at the following website: www. sagepub.co.uk/nezlek

Data preparation

For various reasons, new users of HLM sometimes have difficulty preparing the raw data files for analysis. In anticipation of such problems, I offer the following advice. As noted above, there is a separate data file for each level of analysis in a model. For two-level data there are two files, and for three-level data there are three files.

In the example diary study in which days are treated as nested within persons, there is a file containing the person level measures (one record for each person), and a file containing the diary entries (one record for each day for each person). In the level 2 data file (person level file: Sage-Diary-Example-Level2.sav) there are 98 entries, and in the level 1 data file (day level file: Sage-Diary-Example-Level1. sav) there are 1256 entries. Similarly, if we had 15 classes that had a total of 250 students, there would be 15 records in the level 2 (classroom) file that would contain information about the class, including perhaps teacher characteristics, and there would be 250 records in the level 1 (student) file. For those who do not have ready access to SPSS, I have saved all the files used in the example analyses as tab-delimited text files (the files have the same names and a .dat extension).

It is critical to note that the number of level 1 records (also referred to as units or observations) does not need to be the same for each of the level 2 units of analysis. In the hypothetical classroom study mentioned above, there could be different numbers of students in each class, and similarly, in the example diary study, participants do not have the same number of days of data. Moreover, there is no need to equalize the number of observations for a class or a person by inserting records (students or days) that contain all missing data or eliminate records for classes or persons that have more than a certain number of observations. In fact, one should never insert or eliminate observations. HLM and other multilevel programs take into account the fact that there can be different numbers of level 1 units for each level 2 unit of analysis. This is an important difference between MLM analyses and repeated measures ANOVA in which all units of analysis have to have the same number of observations.

Assuming the data are structured properly, each file needs to be sorted in the same order. In the level 1 file, this means that all the level 1 observations for a level 2 unit of analysis need to be together, and these groups need to be sorted in the same order as the level 2 data. In essence, the program associates the level 2 data with the level 1 data. To illustrate the sorting, the first few lines of the sample diary data files are presented in Table 6. The first three level 2 units (people) are

Table 6   Properly sorted data files for two-level HLM

Level 2		Level 1			
id$	CESD	id$	jdate$	jdate	tri
x001	18	x001	302	302.0	5.33
x002	17	x001	304	304.0	5.33
x003	25	x001	306	306.0	7.00
		x001	307	307.0	5.67
		x001	308	308.0	5.00
		x001	309	309.0	6.33
		x001	310	310.0	7.00
		x001	311	311.0	6.33
		x001	314	314.0	4.33
		x001	315	315.0	4.33
		x001	316	316.0	6.33
		x002	298	298.0	6.00
		x002	299	299.0	6.00
		x002	300	300.0	6.00
		x002	301	301.0	6.33
		x002	304	304.0	4.00
		x002	306	306.0	5.33
		x002	307	307.0	6.00
		x002	308	308.0	6.67
		x002	309	309.0	6.00
		x002	310	310.0	5.67
		x003	298	298.0	6.33
		x003	300	300.0	6.00
		x003	301	301.0	6.67
		x003	302	302.0	5.67
		x003	303	303.0	6.00
		x003	304	304.0	6.00
		x003	305	305.0	6.67
		x003	306	306.0	6.67
		x003	307	307.0	6.00
		x003	308	308.0	5.33
		x003	309	309.0	5.33
		x003	310	310.0	5.00

presented, and then the level 1 units (days) that accompany these level 2 units are presented. For the sake of thoroughness, for diary studies, I also sort the days within each person using the Julian date (jdate), a system in which 1 January is 1, 2 January is 2, and so forth. Such sorting is necessary to create lagged variables. Nevertheless, level 1 units do not have to be sorted within their corresponding level 2 units. For example, it may not be possible to sort persons within groups in a meaningful way. Also, I put the sorting variables at the very beginning of a file. This makes it easier to examine how the data were sorted if that is necessary.

In the HLM program, the sorting variables are referred to as "id" variables, and they link the data across the files for different levels. By tradition, these id variables are alphanumeric (string) variables, but they do not have to be. For reasons that are not always clear to me, in some programs such as SPSS, sorting data using string variables as the sorting variable can be trickier than it would appear to be on the surface. Differences in width, justification, and I frankly don't know what else, appear to influence the sort. Moreover, for these same reasons, entries that appear to be the same may not be. Assuming the data are structured properly (an important assumption), I have found that invariably, the reason people have trouble creating a MDM file has something to do with how the data were sorted. Moreover, HLM does not have very good diagnostics for the creating MDM part of the program.

To add another level of complexity, from time to time, SPSS changes some aspect of its file structure system in ways that make it impossible for HLM to read the files. SSI typically releases an update to fix this very soon after it is discovered. I will not speculate (as others have) about the fact that such problems appear to have become more common after SPSS added a multilevel module to its offerings. I will note that at the time of this writing, SPSS 17 and HLM6.08 do not always "play nice" when it comes to alphanumeric (string) identifier fields. In such instances, it may be easier to create a new, numeric id and use that. In fact, as I was finishing this volume, I was in such a situation, and it caused me to add the next few sentences. I just could not get it to work: HLM kept telling me that there was something wrong with how my data were sorted, and no matter how I read and reread and sorted and resorted the data, I could not get HLM to accept the data. When I created a numeric code (simply the case number), and applied it to the level 1 data (a diary data set like the one we will be discussing), everything was fine – even without resorting.

Finally, the full version of HLM can read a wide variety of data files. The free version can read only ASCII (raw data requiring a FORTRAN format – strongly not recommended), SYSTAT, SPSS for Windows, and SAS transport data files. The instructions that follow assume a Windows OS.

Finally, it is essential to keep in mind that HLM has no capabilities to transform, modify, restructure, change, reconstitute, or rescale data in any way, manner, shape, or form. Any changes to the data at any level of analysis need to be made outside of the program using some other system (e.g., SPSS). For example, if after doing a series of analyses you decide that you want to create a new measure to include in the MDM file, you need to create this measure using whatever system you prefer, and then create a new MDM file that includes the new measure. Just in case you missed it the first time, HLM has no capabilities to transform, modify, restructure, change, reconstitute, or rescale data in any way, manner, shape, or form. Really, none.

The example diary study contains data from a study I conducted, unpublished as I write this volume. Participants provided data online each day for two weeks. For present purposes, we will focus on daily measures of self-esteem and Beck's triad (feelings about self, life, and future) as outcomes and daily events as predictors. Self-esteem was measured with four items corresponding to items 3, 6, 7, and 10 of Rosenberg's classic 1965 measure, and Beck's triad was measured with three items I have used in a series of studies. The outcomes were measured using 1–7 scales, and initially, we will focus on mean daily self-esteem score (i.e., the mean response to the four items, with items 1 and 3 reverse scored). Event scores are "impact scores" – average ratings of events in a category using a 0 (did not happen) to 4 (very important) scale. There are overall positive and negative event scores (POSMN and NEGMN), and positive and negative events are also broken down into social and achievement domains. For details of these measures, see Nezlek (2005). At the person level, we will focus on individual differences in scores on the CESD, a well-known measure of depressive symptoms. CESD scores are represented as both raw (CESD) and standardized (CESDZ) measures, and the interaction of participant sex (variable SEXCNT, a contrast variable, 1 = female, −1 = male) and the standardized CESDZ scores is CESDSX.

Creating a MDM file

To create the MDM file, you open the program, left click on "File," and then click on either "Make new mdm file ..." or "Make new mdm file from old .... " Choose the first if you want to create an entirely new MDM file. Choose the second if you want to use the set of commands that you used to create a previous MDM file to create another MDM file. For me, there are two reasons to use an existing template: adding variables and adding cases. To add variables you simply include the new variables you want included when the program prompts you for the variables to include in the MDM file. If you keep the same file name and add either variables or cases to a file, the program will read the new file with the additional data. We will change an existing file later.

You are then prompted for the type of file input. For present purposes I will assume SPSS files. The default stat package is SPSS. This can be changed by clicking on "File" then "Preferences." In the Preferences box you can also change how the models are presented on the screen and whether you want graph files. And for those of you who are into it, the foreground and background colors can be changed.

Then you have to select the type of file you want to create. This is critical. For standard two-level models you should select HLM2 (e.g., persons within groups, days within persons), and for standard three-level models, you should select HLM3. The next two options, HMLM and HMLM2, are used when the first level of a model is a multivariate model. The HCM2 option is for cross-classified data. The HMLM and HCM options are discussed (briefly) later.

The next panel is where you select the files for each level, name the MDM and MDMT files, indicate how to treat missing data at level 1, and indicate the type of analysis, either persons within groups or measures within persons. This last choice is simply cosmetic. If you select persons within groups, the subscripts in a two-level model will be βs at level 1 and γs at level 2. If you select measures within person, the subscripts will be πs at level 1 and βs at level 2. This is new for HLM6 compared to previous versions. Don't ask me why. The estimates of the coefficients do not vary as a function of this choice (I have created both types of MDM files and compared the results); I assume it has something to do with representing people with βs across different types of models.

For the MDMT file, the suffix ".mdmt" is automatically appended to the name you enter in the MDM template file name box. Cruelly, the suffix ".mdm" is not appended to the name you enter in the MDM file name box. You have to append it yourself. So, you should enter "myfile.mdm" not just "myfile." The program will not be happy if you do not attach the ".mdm." Just do it.

For missing data, select how the program should handle them. Two options are available. (1) Exclude a case from the MDM file if it has a missing value on any of the level 1 variables included in the MDM file. (2) Include all cases, but delete a case from any analysis if there is a missing value on a variable included in that analysis. The advantage of the first option is that all analyses are based upon exactly the same number of observations – an important consideration for some. The advantage of the second option is that the amount of data used in any specific analysis is maximized.

The default setting for missing data at level 1 is "No missing data." If you do not indicate that there are missing data and the program encounters missing data, you will get a message "Missing data found at level 1! Unable to continue." If you indicate that there are missing data, you will need to specify how to handle them (one of the two options mentioned above). Otherwise, you will get a message "Handling of missing data needs to be specified" when you try to save the MDMT file, and you must save the MDMT file to make the MDM file.

Note that there is no option regarding how to treat missing data at level 2 (nor at levels 2 and 3 in a three-level model). In HLM, missing data are not allowed at level 2. If a case at level 2 has a missing value on a variable that is included in the MDM file, the case will not be included in the MDM file. One way to know if you have missing data on a variable that was included in the MDM file is that a message will appear in the STS file: "Group [id field of the case with the missing data] not in level 2 file." In the program window that opens while HLM is running, a message will also appear stating that "x level 2 cases were deleted due to missing data," where "*x*" is the number of cases that were deleted, but such a message will not appear in the STS file (or anywhere else for that matter).

There may be times when the nature and amount of missing data at level 2 (in a two-level model) require the creation of separate MDM files that differ in terms of the number of cases that are included due to missing data. Assume a study in which there are two sets or measures for level 2 cases (e.g., people in a diary study, group leaders or teachers in a person within groups study). For whatever reasons, a substantial number of level 2 cases do not have one of the sets of measures. If a MDM file is created that includes both sets of measures, a substantial number of level 2 units will be deleted from the MDM file, and these cases will not be included in any analysis.

One possible solution to this is to create two MDM files, one that includes only the set of measures that all (or most) level 2 cases have in full, and another that includes only cases that have both sets of measures (which by definition, will be fewer than the number that is missing one set of measures). As is the case with any other type of analysis, there may be concerns about the results based on the smaller set of observations: why are the observations missing, does this reflect some bias, and so forth? One possible solution to this is to include the presence or absence of a set of measures in the analyses based on the larger data set. If there are no differences between the two groups in the coefficients, then at least you can say that whatever the lack of a set of measures represents, it is not associated with the coefficients of interest. In terms of using HLM to do this, see the later section "Using existing MDMT files."

Finally, most times, HLM will "pick up" the missing values used by a stat package. For example if, for some Byzantine reason, an analyst represents missing data with 99 and codes this as part of the file that is saved, HLM should recognize this. Note that I said "most times" and "should." I have worked with data sets in which values that were coded to represent missing data in a save file were read as valid values by HLM. My guess is that this was due to some peculiar combination of a version of HLM and a version of SPSS. Regardless, analysts are strongly encouraged to inspect the STS file to verify how many observations were included in the MDM file and to ensure that no invalid values were read as valid (e.g., no 99s for 1–7 scales).

The next few sections describe and discuss how to use the program, and do this by using the sample data sets. The analyses described in these sections are meant to be done in sequence and more or less at one sitting; however, you can close the program and return at different points. I have included instructions about how to do this at some of these points.

Using the example data

Open the program, click File, click "Make new MDM," select HLM2, and then click Okay. To select the level 1 file, under "Level 1 Specification" click

"Browse," and open the file "Sage-Example-Diary-Level1.sav" from wherever you have it stored. Click "Choose Variables," then select ID$ as the identifying variable by clicking on the ID box. Note that the name ID$ appears in italics, indicating that it is a string variable. To include variables in a file for analyses, click on the box next to the variable "in MDM." Select RSE (the daily self-esteem measure) and POSMN and NEGMN (the mean scores for positive and negative events respectively) and ACHPOSMN and ACHNEGMN (the mean scores for positive and negative achievement events respectively). Click OK. There are some missing data in this data set, so under "Missing Data?" select Yes, and then select "running analyses." To set the level 2 file, go through a similar process. Click "Browse" and open the file "Sage-Example-Diary-Level2.sav." Click "Choose Variables," then select ID$ as the id variable and select CESDZ, CESDSX, and CESD to include in the MDM. Click OK. (The identifying variables in the two files do not have to have the same name; however, the entries themselves have to be the same. For character string variables this includes spaces and justification. For example, the entries "abc" "abc" "abc" and "abc" are different.) Type in the name for the MDM file in the upper right box – use "sagediary.mdm." To finish, click on "Save mdmt file," then enter the name for the file (sagediary) – no need to include the ".mdmt" suffix.

NB: if you realize that you have made a mistake, or you want to change some aspect of the MDM template procedure, make certain that you save the changed template before making the MDM. The program makes the MDM file using the last template you saved.

Next, click "Make MDM." The black "program is running" box should open, some names and numbers will be presented quickly, and before you can read too much, the box will close – sort of like Sperling's early research on iconic memory. The MDM file has been created. Next, click on "Check Stats," and Notepad will open with the HLM2MDM.STS file staring at you. If you do not click on "Check Stats" after the MDM file is created, the program will ask you to do so but will allow you to proceed if you do not. This was not always the case in HLM. I asked the SSI staff why they made users examine the STS file, and they told me that too many people were not examining their STS files and were calling them about problems they could have known about if they had looked at the file. So, you have to click twice anyway, so why not look at it? It is a good idea. STS files contain simple summary statistics and serve as a check that the data you wanted to read or thought had been read into the MDM file were, in fact, read into the file.

HLM writes all files into the directory where you saved the MDMT file. There you will find the MDM file itself (sagediary.mdm), the MDMT file (sagediary.mdmt), the aforementioned HLM2MDM.STS (which, to keep things straight, I would immediately rename sagediary.sts – which is how it appears in the sample data files), and a file named "creatmdm.mdmt." The creatmdm file contains the last set of the "making a MDM file" commands the program used. The STS and

MDMT files are text files and can be opened and inspected with Notepad or any program that can read a simple text file. The MDM file is full of computer gibberish characters and there is no reason to open it. If you open it, all you can do is change it and consequently ruin it. Note that in the sample files, these specific MDM files are located in the folder "Original-MDM."

A quick glance at the MDMT file is instructive. It is a line-by-line summary of the commands and specifications you provided regarding the MDM file. This includes the names of the files, the variables that were selected, missing value options, and so forth. If you have questions about what went into a MDM file, you can usually answer them by consulting the MDMT file. Moreover, as described below, you can use a MDMT file as a basis or starting point for creating another, different MDM file.

Setting up analyses: unconditional model

Once the MDM file is created, analyses can begin. Most multilevel modelers strongly recommend that all variables of interest (either potential dependent or independent variables) should first be analyzed with a "totally unconditional" model, i.e., a model in which there are no predictors at any level of analysis. Such an analysis gives some indication of the distribution of the variance of a measure, and by implication, some indication of "where the action is," i.e., at what level might analyses be more or less fruitful. It is important to note that even if there is relatively little variance at a level of analysis, it may still be possible to find relationships between the dependent measure and predictors. Moreover, for those hell-bent on reporting ICCs (or for those who are required to report them), these variance estimates can be used to estimate ICCs.

In HLM, running an unconditional model requires selecting a variable as the dependent measure, naming the output file (unless one wants to overwrite files constantly), and saving the command file (either under a new name or not). Using the MDM file we just created, click on RSE, and then "Outcome Variable." The screen in front of you should now display the level 1 and level 2 model equations. For an unconditional model, there are no predictors. To name the output file, click on "Basic Settings," then enter the output file name in the blank space. Keeping in mind that HLM will write the output file into the directory into which you save the command file (next step), you do not need to put the full path for the output file. Just a file name will do. There is also an option to provide a title for the analysis. I tend not to use this field, but it is another way in which you can describe what you have done and why. Click OK.

For this sample analysis, I named the output file "rse0.txt." The "rse" represents the outcome measure, the "0" tells me that it is a null model, and the "txt" suffix denotes the fact that HLM output files are simple text files that can be opened with

Notepad. That is my system. You need to use a system that makes sense for you. If you do not specify a name for the output file, the default name is hlm2.txt. For the moment, we will ignore the other fields in the Basic Settings box.

NB: HLM will not ask permission to overwrite an output file. If you specify an output file name that already exists, the program just writes over it, and the original is lost (truly lost, it is pretty much impossible to recover – I guess the CIA could). In many instances, this is adaptive. If you make a mistake or want to change some aspect of the analysis and do not want to keep the original analysis, you write over it with little effort. On the other hand, if you want to keep the original file, you need to rename it or specify a different name in the program.

Next, click on "File," then "Save as." This opens the box where you enter the name for the command file. For this example, I named the file "zero." The full file name is saved as "zero.hlm," but the program appends the ".hlm" suffix. Now, click on "Run Analysis," and the little black "program is running" box should open. Depending upon the complexity of the model, you will see different numbers of iterations that will pass by more slowly or more quickly. Lots of slowly passing iterations mean that the algorithm is having some difficulties estimating a solution. As discussed above, this is often the case when there are bad or weak error terms. Typically, unconditional models converge quickly and take just a few iterations to do so.

Before examining the output, let's examine the command (.hlm) file. By the way, all of the command files for the example analyses are in a folder labeled "Command Files." You can open a command file in Notepad. Like the MDMT file, it is a simple text file, and like the MDMT file, it contains a line-by-line summary of the commands that represent the analysis. Many of the lines concern options that most analysts will rarely if ever use (e.g., a variance known analysis), but the file describes the basics of any analysis (e.g., the MDM file used, the models, the output file). It is possible to edit a HLM file in a text editor and use an edited version, but this is something that analysts should do only after they are quite familiar with the program and how it works. Also, the program always writes a file called "newcmd.hlm," which contains the commands used in the most recent analysis.

Reading the output file: unconditional model

To view the results of analysis (an output file), click on "File," then "View Output." Doing this automatically opens a Notepad window containing the most recent output file. By the way, all the output files for the example analyses are in a folder labeled "Output Files." The first section of the output contains a description of the model: the source of the data, the command and output files, error terms, centering, and other aspects of the analysis. Note that the path names specified in the output files for the example analyses (the specific folders/directories in which a file resides) will differ somewhat from the paths that a file may have on your computer. Nevertheless, the file name itself (the very last part of the full name) will be the same.

The output file is quite thorough, so an analyst should be able to know exactly what was done for a particular analysis. In addition, there are the equations for each level of the model. Admittedly, these equations are not presented in the fancy Greek letters with subscripts that appear in articles and books, but they are perfectly understandable.

Here is the model in the form we have been using:

level 1 (day) $y_{ij} = \beta_{0j} + r_{ij}$
level 2 (person) $\beta_{0j} = \gamma_{00} + \mu_{0j}$

For now, I will skip over the middle of the output and call your attention to the end of the output. For an unconditional model, this is where the most interesting results are to be found, and there are three that are particularly important: the estimated mean (printed G00 for γ_{00}), and the level 2 and level 1 variance estimates (printed U0 and R for μ_0 and r). For our sample data set, the estimated mean is 5.38 (rounded), and the level 2 and level 1 variances (rounded) are .798 and .665 respectively. As discussed previously, the distribution of variances provides a sense of "where the action is" in a data set. For this measure, about 55% of the total variability is at level 2 (between persons) and the remaining variability is at level 1 (the within-person or day level). The ICC would be .55.

As is the case with all coefficients estimated by a HLM analysis, the G00 coefficient is tested against a null of 0, which for this example is not particularly meaningful because the outcome was measured on a 1–7 scale. It is possible, however, to make testing of the intercept *per se* meaningful by using scales that have meaningful 0 points or by transforming a scale to make 0 meaningful. For example, if policy preference was measured using a 1–7 scale with 4 as neutral, if 4 was subtracted from all scores, the significance test of the G00 coefficient would indicate if the average response was significantly different from the midpoint, i.e., favorable or unfavorable.

In the middle of the output, the program presents a reliability estimate. For the analysis just discussed, this estimate is not some type of Cronbach's alpha or measure of the internal consistency of the items that make up the daily self-esteem measure. Rather, the reliability estimates HLM provides are indications of the ratio of true to total variance, a classic definition of reliability. For this particular measure, the reliability of the intercept was .937, which indicates that the mean response (which the intercept represented in this analysis) was quite reliable. A practical implication of this is that it should be relatively easy (statistically) to model individual differences in the intercept because it is highly reliable.

User hint: to see analyses other than the one that was just conducted you need to open another window of some kind (e.g., Notepad). It is possible, however, to open an output file via HLM, leave it open, run a new analysis, and then open the results of the new analysis in a new window while the previous analysis remains open.

Adding a predictor at level 2

The next analysis to be considered is one in which a predictor is added at level 2. To do this, first click on "Level 2" in the upper left hand corner. This switches the variables that are displayed from level 1 to level 2. Then click on CESDZ, and then "uncentered." The variable name CESDZ will appear in the level 2 equation in a normal font. Grand-mean centered predictors appear in italics. Normally, continuous variables at level 2 are entered grand-mean centered, but because CESD scores were standardized prior to analysis, whether CESDZ is entered uncentered or grand-mean centered does not matter.

Next, the output file needs to be renamed (Basic Settings). I named the file rse-cesdz.txt. Next the command file needs to be saved (File, Save as). If you click File, then Save (not Save as), whatever file is in use is overwritten, without asking for permission to do so. I created a new file, "rse-cesdz" (the .hlm is added automatically). If you do not save the command file, the program asks you if you want to, and you can run the model after you say it is okay not to save the command file.

At the outset, I recommend saving individual command files because it makes it easy to retrace one's steps or to redo analyses with minor changes. When I am doing a lot of analyses that have the same structure (e.g., same level 1 and level 2 predictors for multiple outcome measures), I keep a copy of a HLM file that represents that model.

Here is this model in the form that we have been using:

level 1 (day)　　$y_{ij} = \beta_{0j} + r_{ij}$

level 2 (person)　$\beta_{0j} = \gamma_{00} + \gamma_{01} (CESDZ) + \mu_{0j}$

The G01 coefficient (γ_{01}) represents the relationship between CESD z-scores and mean daily self-esteem. In this case, the coefficient of $-.512$ (rounded) is significantly different from 0. The t-ratio (which is not a true t-test but an approximate t-distribution) is 6.247, which is significant at the .0001 level. By the way, the negative signs of t-ratios can be ignored. The coefficient is interpreted this way: for every 1 unit increase in CESD scores, average daily self-esteem decreased by .512. Because CESD scores had been standardized, this means that the G01 coefficient represented the change in the outcome measure associated with a 1 SD increase in CESD scores. One of the advantages of standardizing level 2 scores is that it makes it easier to calculate predicted values that are ±1 SD.

Earlier, I mentioned some caveats about using changes in variance estimates to estimate effect sizes in MLM. With this in mind, here is how to describe the relationship between CESD z-scores and daily self-esteem in terms of changes in variances.

The variance of the intercept from the unconditional analyses of self-esteem was .798. The variance of the intercept from this analysis is .544 (rounded). This represents a 32% reduction in variance (.798 − .544) / .798), which could also be expressed as a correlation of .56 (the square root of .32). In this situation, i.e., a single level 2 predictor of a level 1 intercept with no level 1 predictors, my sense is that such an estimate is pretty stable.

To illustrate the impact that standardizing has, the above analysis can be repeated by including raw CESD scores at level 2 instead of CESD z-scores. The output for this analysis is in the file "rse-cesd-grandc.txt" and the command file is "rse-cesd-grandc." As can be seen from this file, the *t*-ratio for the CESD raw scores is exactly the same as it was when z-scores were used. Because the coefficients that are produced when z-scores are used at level 2 are easier to interpret than when raw scores are included at level 2, in the examples that follow, when CESD scores are included in an analysis, the standardized score was used.

Changing centering

To change the centering of a variable, it needs to be removed from the model and re-entered with the new centering option. To continue the previous example, with the program open, display the level 2 variables (click on Level 2), select CESDZ and select "Delete variable from model." Then click on CESDZ again and select "Add variable grand centered." Note that the font that is used to display CESDZ is now italics. To keep things clear, rename the output file "rse-cesdz-grandc.txt" and save the command file as "rse-cesdz-grandc." Run the analysis. By the way, the same procedure (removal and re-entry) is needed to change the centering of level 1 predictors.

As always, at the beginning of the output the model is described. Note that for this analysis, in the description of the fixed effects (just below the phrase "The model specified for the fixed effects was:"), there is a $ symbol next to the CESDZ coefficient, and the coefficient is noted as having been grand centered. To appreciate this, compare this part of the output to the output of the previous analysis when CESDZ was entered uncentered: there is no symbol next to the CESDZ coefficient in that output. Note also that the results of the two analyses are exactly the same because CESDZ was standardized (meaning the mean was 0 − see the STS file), and so in this case, grand-mean and zero centering (or uncentered) are the same.

Adding a predictor at level 1

Adding predictors to a level 1 model follows the same procedure as adding level 2 predictors. Let's start with an unconditional model. If the program is still open from the analyses above, delete the CESDZ score at level 2. To delete the variable, click on Level 2, select CESDZ, and select "Delete variable from model."

If the program is not open from before, open it, click on File, then select "Edit/ run old command ...." Select the zero.hlm command file (if you saved it). If you did not save it, click on File, then select "Create a model using an existing ..." and select the MDM file that was created before. If you choose the last option, you will have the same screen that you had right after the MDM file was created, and you should click on RSE and select it as an outcome measure.

To add a level 1 predictor, click on the level 1 variable you want to include and then select a centering option. For this example, select POSMN (mean of positive events) and select "Add variable group-mean centered." POSMN will now appear in level 1 equation in a bold font. As was the case with level 2 predictors, the font used to display a predictor indicates how it was centered: standard font for no centering (zero centered), bold font for group-mean centered, italics for grand-mean centered.

By default, level 1 predictors are entered as fixed; no random error term is estimated. This is a change in HLM6 from previous versions. I asked the folks at SSI about why the default for a random coefficient modeling program was to model coefficients as not randomly varying, and they told me that it was because too many users were running models with too many predictors at level 1. As discussed in Chapter 2 in the section "Building a model," this meant that the models were "blowing up" too often (not converging or running at all), so SSI fixed this problem by fixing the predictors (sorry, could not resist). I don't think this was the best solution, but it's their program.

Regardless, to include a random error term, click on the equation for the coefficient with which you are concerned. The equation will now be highlighted (in the default color scheme this will be a pale yellow). Then click on the error term itself. Error terms that are included are presented in a normal font. Error terms that are not included are presented in a faint (very light gray) font.

To finish, name the output file (Basic Settings) and then save the command file (click File, Save as). I will use the name "rse-posmn.txt" for the output file and "rse-posmn" for the command file. By the way, I organize my analyses by naming output files using index levels. The first index of the output file name indicates the outcome variable, and the proceeding indices represent predictors, first level 1 then level 2. You will need to use a naming system that makes sense to you. Run analysis. The little black "program is running" box will open. Note that there are a few more iterations than before. This is because more parameters are being estimated. Here is the model in the form that we have been using:

level 1 (day) $\qquad y_{ij} = \beta_{0j} + \beta_{1j} (\text{POSMN}) + r_{ij}$

level 2 (person) $\quad \beta_{0j} = \gamma_{00} + \mu_{0j}$

$\qquad\qquad\qquad\ \beta_{1j} = \gamma_{10} + \mu_{1j}$

Inspect the output (click File, View output). The beginning of the output file has the basic data about the model and the analysis. Note that in the section of the output beginning with "The model specified for the fixed effects ..." the coefficient for POSMN is accompanied by an *. As noted in the program, this indicates that the coefficient was entered as group-mean centered. Similar to the notation for level 2 predictors, at level 1, uncentered predictors have no accompanying symbol or description, and grand-mean centered predictors are accompanied by $ and are noted as having been grand-mean centered.

Before evaluating the fixed effects (the coefficients testing whether relationships are significantly different from 0), I always examine the random error terms. As discussed previously, the accuracy of the estimates and the tests of the fixed effects depends upon the accuracy of the modeling of the random effects. For this particular analysis, the random error term for the POSMN slope was significantly different from 0: look at the last part of the output, chi-squared of 202.6 (rounded), $p < .000$. This means that POSMN should be modeled as randomly varying.

Also note a minor change in the estimate of the variance of the intercept. In the unconditional model it was .79770. In this analysis, it is .80653. Substantively, there should be no change in the intercept when predictors are group-mean centered; the intercept is the expected value for an observation that is at the mean score for all predictors in a group, which is what it was without any predictors. The difference between these two variance estimates (how much the intercept varies across the groups, in our case people) is simply a sort of rounding error difference that is of no consequence.

The hypothesis that the within-person (day level) relationship between POSMN and RSE is significantly different from 0 is tested by the G10 (γ_{10}) coefficient. As noted earlier, HLM provides two sets of estimated coefficients, robust and non-robust, and because we can use the robust estimates in this analysis, we will focus on those. The G10 coefficient is .554, which is significantly different from 0 ($t = 7.799, p < .000$). This coefficient is interpreted as follows. On average, for every 1.0 increase in POSMN, RSE increases .554. The emphasis for "on average" reflects the fact that this is a mean of the within-person relationship between POSMN and RSE, and because the random error term is significantly different from 0, we know that this relationship varies across level 2 units (i.e., people). Keep in mind that if the random error term was not significant, it might still be possible to model individual differences in the slope by including predictors at level 2.

Another way to describe this relationship would be to estimate the effect size expressed in terms of reductions in variance. The level 1 variance from the unconditional model was .665. The level 1 variance in this analysis was .562 (rounded). Applying the same logic as was applied to estimating effect sizes for level 2 predictors, the reduction in variance was 15% (.665 − .562) / .665). This corresponds to a correlation of about .39 (square root of .15). This correlation is basically an estimate of the average within-person correlation between RSE and POSMN.

NB: as discussed previously, the type of variance reduction procedure described above can be used only when level 1 predictors are group-mean centered. They cannot be used when level 1 predictors are grand-mean centered. Moreover, for reasons that I have not been able to determine, estimates of such correlations are not symmetrical. For example, if a set of models are run that parallel those above in which POSMN is the dependent measure and RSE is the predictor (posmn0.txt and posmn-rse.txt), the variance reduced in POSMN by RSE is 12%, and the estimated correlation is .35. My experience is that such asymmetries are typically not that large (on the order of the difference in the present example), but they are not 0. Conversations about such asymmetries with those more knowledgeable than myself have suggested that the asymmetries may have something to do with differences between the variables in the distribution of variance across levels of analysis, but I know of no definitive explanation.

Another way to describe or explain such relationships is to estimate predicted values for the outcome for observations that are ±1 SD on the predictor, a standard procedure in regression-based analyses. Within the multilevel context, it is critical to keep in mind that the SD of a level 1 variable that is provided in a STS file is not the appropriate SD to use for such estimates. It is inaccurate because the SD from the STS file is based on a "flat file" – a file that does not take the grouped nature of observations into account.

The level 1 SD for a measure should be based on the level 1 variance obtained from a totally unconditional model of the predictor. The level 1 variance of POSMN was .220, and the estimated SD was .469. (See output labeled "posmn0.txt"). So, the estimated self-esteem on a day in which positive events were 1 SD above and below the mean for positive events is calculated as follows:

$+1$ SD: $y = 5.382 + .554 (.469) = 5.641$
-1 SD: $y = 5.382 + .554 (-.469) = 5.122$

Predictors at both levels of analysis

To me, the ability to model level 1 differences in slopes is one of the most interesting aspects of MLM and one of its most powerful advantages over other types of analyses. As discussed above, various terms are used to describe such modeling (e.g., cross-level interaction, slopes as outcomes), but regardless of the term, to me, such relationships are where a lot of "the action is" in terms of the ability of MLM to advance our understanding of social and personality psychological phenomena. For example, finding that your self-esteem is higher on days when more good things happen to you than it is on days when fewer good things happen is interesting, but to be able to model or explain who fluctuates more in terms of this adds meaningfully to our understanding of the basic relationship. In terms of advancing our understanding, such interactions serve purposes similar to the purposes served by interactions within experimental paradigms – establishing limiting or facilitating conditions for a baseline relationship that expands our understanding of these baseline relationships.

In terms of the ongoing example with which we have been concerned, we can illustrate such analyses by adding CESD scores at level 2 to the model we just examined. Assuming the program is still open with a level 1 model in which RSE is being predicted by POSMN (group-mean centered), we simply add CESDZ to each of the level 2 equations. If the program is not open, open it, and either select a previous command (HLM) file to modify, or select the MDM file and set up the model.

To add a predictor to a level 2 equation, click on the equation to which you want to add the predictor (exactly as we did to add the error term), and then click on the predictor (CESDZ) from the menu of level 2 variables and add it uncentered (because it has already been centered). As discussed in the section on model building in Chapter 2, the same predictors should be added to each level 2 equation. Name the output (click Basic Settings, I used "rse-posmn-cesdz.txt"), save the file (File, Save as, I used "rse-posmn-cesdz"). Run the analysis. Little black box opens for not too long. Adding a level 2 predictor does not add much difficulty to the estimation procedure. Here is the model in the form that we have been using:

level 1 (day) $\quad y_{ij} = \beta_{0j} + \beta_{1j} (POSMN) + r_{ij}$

level 2 (person) $\quad \beta_{0j} = \gamma_{00} + \gamma_{01} (CESDZ) + \mu_{0j}$

$\beta_{1j} = \gamma_{10} + \gamma_{11} (CESDZ) + \mu_{1j}$

As always, the beginning of the output contains the model specifications. Nothing new here. Pro forma, I check the error terms. Also nothing new there. The fixed effects tell the story. The relationship between the intercept and CESDZ is very similar to what it was in the analysis when we had an unconditional model at level 1 (only the intercept) and predicted that intercept with CESDZ (−.512347 now, −.511781 then). Conceptually, the intercept has not changed from that analysis. When predictors are entered group-mean centered, the intercept remains the group mean, which is what the intercept represents when there are no predictors. The slight difference between the analyses in the relationships between CESDZ and the intercept is due to the fact that all the coefficients in an analysis are estimated simultaneously, and so a change in one part of a model can change estimates in another part.

A similar and unimportant difference between this model and one of the earlier models is the estimate of the intercept of the slope (i.e., the mean slope, the G10 coefficient). In the previous model (rse-posmn.txt) the mean slope was .554298. In this analysis, because CESDZ was entered uncentered and it was standardized, the intercept of the slope should not have changed. When a predictor is entered uncentered, the slope represents the expected value when a predictor is 0 (the mean in our case). The intercept of the slopes in this analysis was .549791, not exactly the same as before. Once again, the difference between these estimates is a function of the other coefficients being estimated in the model, a sort of rounding error that is not meaningful.

The new information in this analysis is the relationship between CESD scores and the slope representing the relationship between self-esteem and positive events. This is tested by the G11 (γ_{11}) coefficient. This coefficient (.219, rounded) is significantly different from 0 ($t = 3.70, p < .001$). Substantively, this means that the relationship between self-esteem and positive events varied as a function of people's reports of depression. More specifically, this moderating relationship can be interpreted in the same way the G01 coefficient (the relationship between CESD and the intercept) was interpreted.

The most direct way to understand this moderating relationship is to estimate predicted values for people ±1 SD. These estimates are as follows:

+1 SD: $y = .549 + .219 (1.0) = .768$

−1 SD: $y = .549 + .219 (−1.0) = .330$

These estimated values show that the relationship between self-esteem and positive events is stronger for people who have higher scores on the CESD. This moderating relationship can also be explained in terms of reductions in the variance of the slope. The variance of the slope from the original analysis (rse-posmn. txt) was .233. The variance of the slope when the CESD was included at level 2 was .186. This corresponds to a reduction of variance of approximately 20%, ($.233 − .186) / .233$).

NB: it is critical to keep in mind two aspects of modeling differences in slopes. First, as discussed previously, level 2 differences in a level 1 slope can be modeled when the random error term for a slope is not significant or is not modeled. Curious readers may want to repeat the slopes as outcomes analyses just described with the random error terms for the slopes deleted. They will find the results (mean slopes and the moderating effects of CESDZ) of those analyses to be quite similar to the results that were presented. To some extent, this raises the question of how important the error terms are. As discussed before, error terms need to be specified properly to maximize the accuracy of the tests of fixed effects, even though the error terms themselves may not be meaningful. Sometimes the absence or presence of error terms does not matter for tests of fixed effects, whereas other times it does. Decisions about modeling error should not include the ramifications of such decisions for the results of the tests of fixed effects. Run the model, then check the error terms. If they are all significant (or close to significant), keep them, and look at the fixed effects. If error terms need to be deleted, delete them, re-run the model and then look at the error terms. Repeat until the error structure is stabilized, i.e., all the error terms that are included are significant, then (finally) examine the fixed effects.

Interactions at level 2

It is also possible to examine interactions at level 2. In the sample data set there is a variable named CESDZSX that represents the interaction of CESD and a contrast-coded sex variable SEXCNT (1 = female, −1 = male). The model below examined if the relationship between self-esteem and achievement events varied as a joint function of sex and CESD scores. Achievement events are represented by ACHPOSMN and ACHNEGMN (positive and negative). By now, you should be able to set this model up, but the command file is "rse-achpos-achneg-cesdz-sex.txt" and the output file is "rse-achpos-achneg-cesdz-sex.hlm" if you are feeling a little needy.

level 1 (day) $\quad y_{ij} = \beta_{0j} + \beta_{1j} (\text{ACHPOSMN}) + \beta_{2j} (\text{ACHNEGMN}) + r_{ij}$

level 2 (person) $\quad \beta_{0j} = \gamma_{00} + \gamma_{01} (\text{SEXCNT}) + \gamma_{02} (\text{CESDZ}) + \gamma_{03} (\text{CESDZSX}) + \mu_{0j}$

$\qquad\qquad\qquad \beta_{1j} = \gamma_{10} + \gamma_{11} (\text{SEXCNT}) + \gamma_{12} (\text{CESDZ}) + \gamma_{13} (\text{CESDZSX}) + \mu_{1j}$

$\qquad\qquad\qquad \beta_{2j} = \gamma_{20} + \gamma_{21} (\text{SEXCNT}) + \gamma_{22} (\text{CESDZ}) + \gamma_{23} (\text{CESDZSX}) + \mu_{2j}$

This analysis indicated that the slope between self-esteem and negative achievement events (the third equation at level 2) varied as a joint function of sex and CESD scores – the γ_{23} was significant. A straightforward way to interpret this interaction is to estimate predicted scores for men and women who are ±1 SD on the CESD. This is done as follows. The coefficient for the intercept of the slope γ_{20} is −.61. The sex contrast coefficient γ_{21} is +.15, the CESDZ coefficient γ_{22} is +.03, and the coefficient for the interaction term γ_{23} is −.19. "Plugging" values into the equation to generate predicted scores yields the following. Keep in mind that the value of the interaction term is calculated by multiplying the values for the contrast code and the CESD score.

female–low	$-.61 + .15 \times (+1) + .03 \times (-1) + (-.19) \times (-1) = -.30$
female–high	$-.61 + .15 \times (+1) + .03 \times (+1) + (-.19) \times (+1) = -.62$
male–low	$-.61 + .15 \times (-1) + .03 \times (-1) + (-.19) \times (+1) = -.98$
male–high	$-.61 + .15 \times (-1) + .03 \times (+1) + (-.19) \times (-1) = -.54$

These predicted values show that the interaction was due to the fact that for women, increases in CESD scores were associated with stronger (more negative) slopes between self-esteem and negative achievement events. For men, the opposite relationship existed: increases in CESD scores were associated with weaker (less negative) slopes.

Group-mean versus grand-mean centering at level 1

Although the present data set conceptually calls for group-mean centered predictors, events can be entered grand-mean centered to illustrate the impact that changing the centering of a level 1 predictor can have on parameter estimates. Start with RSE as the outcome measure with no predictors at either level of analysis. Add POSMN grand-mean centered. Toggle the error term to make the coefficient randomly varying. I named the output "rse-posmn-grandc.txt" and the command file "rse-posmn-grandc." Run analysis.

At the top of the output, you will see that POSMN is now accompanied with a % sign and a note indicating that it was grand-mean centered. Moving to the end of the output, note the variance estimates. The variance of the intercept is .71113, whereas when POSMN was entered group-mean centered, it was .80653. This difference in variances reflects the difference between the analyses in what the intercept represents. When POSMN was entered group-mean centered, the intercept was functionally equivalent to the intercept from an unconditional model. It was the expected score for an observation that was at the group mean for a predictor, and accordingly, the variance of the intercept from that analysis was the same as the variance from an unconditional model (.79770).

When POSMN was entered grand-mean centered, the intercept for each group represented the expected value for an observation in each group that was at the grand mean of POSMN. In essence, when a predictor is entered grand-mean centered, the intercept is adjusted for between-group differences in predictors. This adjustment is reflected in the difference between the two analyses in the estimate of the mean RSE (G00). When POSMN was entered group-mean centered, G00 was 5.382494, functionally the same as the mean from the unconditional model (5.382423). When POSMN was entered grand-mean centered, the mean (G00) was 5.433493, not a large difference, but still a difference.

The estimates of parameters for the slopes also differ between the two sets of analyses. The mean slope (G10) from the group-mean centered analysis was .554298, whereas it was .516581 when POSMN was grand-mean centered, and of course, as a function of this, the exact details of the significance tests differed. The estimated random variance of the slope also changed from .23354 (group mean) to .23448 (grand mean).

My experience (and that of other modelers) is that estimates of parameters for intercepts change more as a function of centering options than estimates of parameters of slopes. Of all the parameters that were estimated, the variance of the intercept was the one that changed the most as a function of how POSMN was centered. Moreover, in the present example, how POSMN was centered did not matter substantively in terms of what would probably be the focus of most hypotheses. The estimates of the intercepts and slopes from the two analyses were very similar. Note, however, that this may not always be the case. Sometimes changing centering options can change the substantive conclusions of an analysis. Such a possibility highlights the importance of making decisions about centering carefully, taking into account differences in what coefficients represent as a function of how predictors are centered, and doing so before testing hypotheses.

Using existing MDMT files

One of the advantages of the MDMT file is that it can be reused to serve as the basis for a new MDM file or to modify an existing file. Here are some insights into how to do this. Each option starts as follows. Open the program. Click on File. Select "Make new MDM from old MDM template (.mdmt) file." Select the MDMT file that you want to use. To keep things clear, before redoing the MDM file, you may want to move the original MDM files (.mdm, .mdmt, .sts) to a new folder. In the example data, they were moved to a folder "Original-MDM." Otherwise, you will need to rename the old files, or they will be overwritten.

1 To add cases to an existing file (with no changes in file names or variable names), you can simply rerun the Make MDM command and it will "update" the MDM file with the new cases. When making a MDM file you do not need to specify how many cases are in a file. The program reads whatever is in the file. Of course, if you add level 1 observations for "new" (additional) level 2 units of analysis, you will need to add level 2 units to the level 2 data file.

2 To add variables to a MDM file using the same files as you did originally, click on the "Choose Variables" box for the file from which you want to add the variables. Select the new variables by clicking on the "in MDM" box for the variables you want to add. For our purposes, add the remaining level 1 variables, being certain to include SOCPOSMN and SOCNEGMN (the mean scores for positive and negative social events respectively). Note that HLM will retain variables that have the same name as they did in the previous file, even if they are in a different position in the raw data file. So, if you add a variable to an existing file and save that file under the same name, it will appear in the variable list (in the order in which it appears in the file) but the "in MDM" box will be blank. The program does not include variables by their order in a list. It includes variables by reading variable names, so variables that have been added to a data file after the previous MDM file was created will need to be selected.

3 To change one of the files, click on the "Browse" box corresponding to the level of the data you want to change. Select "Choose variables," include the variables you want to include in the new MDM file, and proceed as below.

If you change anything about the MDM file (i.e., options 2 and 3), you will be asked to save the MDMT file. Depending upon the nature of the changes, you may want to rename the MDM file and save the changed MDMT file under a different name. Regardless, keep in mind that when you add variables (or cases) you may be adding missing values. For level 1 files, this is not a problem *per se*, as long as you have indicated when creating the MDM file that there are missing data and how they should be handled. At level 2, if you include variables for which some cases have missing values, then those cases will be excluded from the new MDM file. Similarly, if you add cases that have missing values on variables that are included in the MDM file, these cases will not be included. Note that although the program requests permission to overwrite a MDMT file, it does not request permission to overwrite a MDM file.

Comparing two coefficients

One of the strengths of MLM is the ability to compare coefficients. Such comparisons can serve a multitude of purposes, and the following analyses illustrate just a small sample of such applications. We will start with a simple comparison: are two coefficients different? Keep in mind that the procedures I illustrate here can be used to compare any coefficients (or sets of coefficients) in a model.

Using the new MDM file just created, select RSE as the outcome measure. Select SOCPOSMN and ACHPOSMN as level 1 predictors and enter each group-mean centered. Toggle the error term for each to make them randomly varying (click on the equation for a coefficient, and the error term should be presented in normal v. faint font). The question of interest concerns the relative strength of the relationship between self-esteem and positive social events (SOCPOSMN) and positive achievement events (ACHPOSMN). Here is the model in the form we have been using:

level 1 (day) $y_{ij} = \beta_{0j} + \beta_{1j} (\text{SOCPOSMN}) + \beta_{2j} (\text{ACHPOSMN}) + r_{ij}$

level 2 (person) $\beta_{0j} = \gamma_{00} + \mu_{0j}$

                      $\beta_{1j} = \gamma_{10} + \mu_{1j}$

                      $\beta_{2j} = \gamma_{20} + \mu_{2j}$

The critical comparison is examined by using what are referred to as tests of fixed effects. Formally, these are tests of constraints on a model. If a constraint leads to a significantly poorer fit of a model (i.e., the constraint is inconsistent with the data), the coefficients compared in a constraint are significantly different. To implement such a comparison, click on "Other Settings," then "Hypothesis Testing." A dialog box will appear that will have 24 boxes in it, each of which can be used to test a different hypothesis (i.e., set of constraints). Click on box 1. You will see a list of all of the coefficients (the γs) in the model.

The equality of the two slopes can be compared by constraining them to be equal. This is done by entering a 1 for one slope in the appropriate box and -1 for the other slope. The specific coefficients being compared are the intercepts of the slopes, in this case, the mean slope for SOCOSMN and ACPOSMN (γ_{10} and γ_{20} respectively). If constraining the two coefficients to be the same (if assuming the difference between them is 0) does not affect the fit of the model, then there is no basis to conclude the slopes are different. This particular hypothesis is tested with a 1 df chi-squared.

I named the output for this analysis "rse-socpos-achpos.txt" and the command file "rse-socpos-achpos". By now, you should be familiar with the introductory part of the output, so we will skip that. Going to the end of the output to check the random error terms reveals that they are all significant. Fine.

Just before the presentation of the variance components is the presentation of the tests of the hypotheses. This is under the heading "Results of General Linear Hypothesis Testing". This table displays the hypotheses that were tested (i.e., the contrasts that were applied to each coefficient, γ_{10} and γ_{20}) and the test of each hypothesis. Constraining the intercepts of the two slopes to be equal resulted in a more poorly fitting model (χ^2 (1) = 4.994, $p < .05$), hence we can conclude that the means of the two slopes are not the same. Or in everyday English (not "statlish"), we can conclude that the slopes are different.

The process can be applied to the negative events. First, delete the two positive events. Click on the SOCPOSMN in the list of variables and select "Delete variable from model". Repeat for ACHPOSMN. Then enter SOCNEGMN and ACHNEGMN as predictors (group-mean centered), toggle the error terms, and constrain the intercepts of the slopes to be equal using the same procedures as before. The results of this analysis are in the output named "rse-socneg-achneg.txt," As can be seen from that output, these two slopes were not different from each other (χ^2 (1) = .151, n.s.).

Comparing moderating relationships

One of our previous analyses found that CESD scores moderated the relationships (slopes) between self-esteem and positive events without distinguishing social and achievement events. The analyses immediately above found that the relationship between self-esteem and positive social events was stronger than the relationship between self-esteem and positive achievement events. Taken together, these findings raise the question: do CESD scores moderate the relationship between self-esteem and positive social events differently than how they moderate the relationship between self-esteem and positive achievement events? In other words, is the cross-level interaction the same for both social events and achievement events?

To answer this question we can set up the following model. Select RSE as the outcome measure. Enter SOCPOSMN and ACHPOSMN group-mean centered and toggle the error terms to make them randomly varying. Add CESDZ (uncentered) to each equation. Here is the model in the form we have been using:

level 1 (day) $\quad y_{ij} = \beta_{0j} + \beta_{1j}(\text{SOCPOSMN}) + \beta_{2j}(\text{ACHPOSMN}) + r_{ij}$

level 2 (person) $\quad \beta_{0j} = \gamma_{00} + \gamma_{01}(\text{CESDZ}) + \mu_{0j}$

$\beta_{1j} = \gamma_{10} + \gamma_{11}(\text{CESDZ}) + \mu_{1j}$

$\beta_{2j} = \gamma_{20} + \gamma_{21}(\text{CESDZ}) + \mu_{2j}$

Click on "Other Settings," then "Hypothesis Testing," and then box 1. Enter a 1 in the box for the coefficient representing the moderating relationship of CESD on social event slopes (SOCPOSMN slope, CESDZ, γ_{11}), and −1 in the box for the coefficient representing the moderating relationship of CESD on achievement event slopes (ACHPOSMN slope, CESDZ, γ_{21}). I named the output file "rse-socpos-achpos-cesdz.txt" and the command file "rse-socpos-achpos-cesdz.hlm."

This analysis did not suggest that the moderating relationship of the CESD varied as a function of the type of positive event being considered. The moderating relationship for social events (γ_{11}) was .129, which was significantly different from 0 ($t = 3.226$, $p < .001$), and the moderating relationship for achievement events (γ_{21}) was .085, which was also significantly different from 0 ($t = 2.04$, $p < .05$). As can be seen from the output, these two slopes were not different from each other ($x^2(1) < 1$, n.s.).

Comparing the strength of coefficients with different signs

The previous examples concerned comparisons of coefficients that were the same sign. The slopes for the two types of positive events were both positive, and the slopes for the two types of negative events were both negative. The moderating relationships of the CESD for social and achievement events were also both positive. Nevertheless, it is also possible to compare the absolute size of two coefficients that differ in sign. Such an analysis could answer a question such as: do negative events influence self-evaluation more than positive events? The procedures used above (simply constraining the coefficients to be the same) do not address such a question, because if two slopes are the same size but are on opposite sides of 0 they might be statistically different (e.g., −.50 and +.50) because of the differences in sign *per se*.

When two coefficients have different signs, their absolute value (strength) can be compared by using a constraint of +1 and +1. Admittedly, this is an unusual type of constraint (most times, the numbers in a constraint sum to 0), but the logic is sound. Think of a constraint in terms of testing some type of weighted sum against the hypothesis that the sum is 0. For two coefficients with the same sign, this would mean weighting one coefficient by 1 and the other by −1. If the two were exactly the same, this weighted sum would be 0. Usually, two coefficients are not exactly the same (if they are, no test is needed), so a test of a constraint tests whether the weighted sum is significantly different from 0. If there are three coefficients and you wanted to compare the first to the average of the second two, you could assign weights of +2 and −1, −1. If this weighted sum was 0 (e.g., +.50 v. +.50 and +.50) you would conclude that the first did not differ from the average of the second and third.

Hypothesis tests all concern whether some estimate is 0 or not. So, when two coefficients have different signs, to compare the absolute values, we need to make a sum of 0 meaningful. If we had a positive and a negative coefficient and simply added them, if they were the same strength, the sum would be 0 (e.g., +.50 and −.50). If they differed (e.g., +.25 and −.50), the sum would not be 0 (−.25 for these two), and we would need to know if this non-zero value was significantly different from 0 or was due to chance fluctuations in the data (the eternal question). To sum two coefficients using weights, we simply assign a weight of 1 to each coefficient.

Back to our sample data set, and the question, "Is the Bad stronger than the Good?" Select RSE as the outcome variable (if it is not already selected). Delete any predictors that may be left over from previous analyses. Enter POSMN and NEGMN as group-mean centered predictors. Toggle the error term for each to make them random. Click "Other Settings," then "Hypothesis Testing." Click on box 1, and enter +1 (or just 1) in the space next to POSMN slope and 1 in the space next to NEGMN slope. Click OK, then OK again to close the "Other Settings" box. I named the output file "rse-posmn-negmn.txt" and the command file "rse-posmn-negmn." Run analysis.

Skip the introductory sections. Go to the variance estimates at the bottom of the output (the true "bottom line" for me). The error terms for both slopes are significant, so we can proceed. Both slopes are different from 0. Note that the POSMN slope is .463, whereas when POSMN was entered alone, it was .554. Similar to OLS regression, adding a predictor to a model can change coefficients. Right now, I cannot recommend a way of testing whether the change from .554 to .463 is significant, although I am working on it. Once again, the tests of fixed effects hypotheses are presented just above the variance estimates. This test found that the slopes were not the same strength (χ^2 (1) = 13.47, $p < .001$). Bad wins.

By the way, you may have noticed that whenever you change the predictors in a model, the "Hypothesis Testing" boxes are all reset to 0. So, whenever you add or delete a predictor (at either level) you have to re-enter any and all constraints even if the comparisons do not involve a variable that has changed. To some extent, this can be circumvented by directly editing the command file (.hlm file) in a text editor such as Notepad; however, I urge you to become familiar with the program before fooling around with .hlm files. You can't break anything by specifying an inappropriate set of commands; however, you may inadvertently change centering options, miss random error terms, and the like. I have been using HLM for 15+ years; yet, rarely do I edit a command file directly in this way.

Three-level analysis with a measurement level as the first level: estimating reliability

As mentioned in Chapter 3 in the section on understanding reliability, you can estimate item level reliabilities for nested data by adding a level of nesting in which items are nested within another level of measurement (e.g., occasions for a diary style data set, or persons when persons are nested within groups). In the example data set with which we have been dealing, the daily measure of self-esteem was measured with four items, and in the previous analyses the outcome was the mean response to these items. All the files pertaining to these analyses are in the folder "Item-Level."

Preparing the data for these analyses required creating an additional data set, which is named "rse-item.sav." The first few lines of this data set are presented in Table 7. There are a few critical elements to setting up a three-level analysis in

Table 7

Item level data file: single variable

id$	jdate$	resp	seq
x001	302	6	1
x001	302	6	2
x001	302	6	3
x001	302	6	4
x001	304	4	1
x001	304	5	2
x001	304	5	3
x001	304	5	4
x001	306	2	1
x001	306	6	2
x001	306	6	3
x001	306	7	4

Item level data file: two variables

id$	jdate$	resp	rse	tri	seq
x001	302	6	1	0	1
x001	302	6	1	0	2
x001	302	6	1	0	3
x001	302	6	1	0	4
x001	302	6	0	1	5
x001	302	5	0	1	6
x001	302	5	0	1	7
x001	304	4	1	0	1
x001	304	5	1	0	2
x001	304	5	1	0	3
x001	304	5	1	0	4
x001	304	6	0	1	5
x001	304	5	0	1	6
x001	304	5	0	1	7
x001	306	2	1	0	1
x001	306	6	1	0	2
x001	306	6	1	0	3
x001	306	7	1	0	4
x001	306	7	0	1	5
x001	306	7	0	1	6
x001	306	7	0	1	7

general and to setting up an item level data set in particular. For an item level data set, each line (each entry) represents a specific response. So, in the sample data presented in the table, for each day (i.e., for each occasion of measurement) there are four observations (four lines of data), one for each of the four items that were used to measure self-esteem each day. If the data were originally entered so that one line contained the data for one day (the usual format), the data will need to be "restructured." How to do this varies from program to program, but most packages will have some way of converting variables into cases or some process that is named something along those lines. There is a code included to represent the item number (column labeled seq). Also, as discussed earlier, similar to a "regular" analysis of reliability, any items that need to be reverse scored should be reversed before creating the MDM file.

Note that there are two identifying fields. One identifier (jdate$) links the level 1 data (item data) to the level 2 data (the day level file, which was level 1 in the previous analyses), and the other identifier (id$) links the level 1 and 2 data to the level 3 data (the person level file, which was level 2 in the previous example). Just as was the case for the two-level analyses we did before, the data need to be sorted in the same order in all files. Although it is not needed, I also sorted the level 1 file (now the item level file) by the item number (seq). A place for everything, and everything in its place.

NB: the two identifying fields need to be the same type of variable – either both character or both numeric. In the original two-level analyses, the jdate field was not used as an identifier, so it did not matter if it was a character or numeric variable. In anticipation of this three-level analysis, I included a character "version" of the jdate variable in the day level file (jdate$).

Creating the MDM file for this analysis follows the same steps as before, with the critical difference that we are now reading in three files instead of two. Open the program: select "File," "Make new mdm file," "Stat package input." Select HLM3 (not HMLM2). For the level 1 file, select "rse-item-save." Click "Choose variables": select ID$ to be the L3id (level 3 id), select JDATE$ to be the L2id (level 2 id), and select RSE to be in the MDM. For the level 2 file, select "Sage-Example-Diary-Level1.sav": select ID$ to be the L3id, select JDATE$ to be the L2id, and select POSMAN to be in the MDM. Note that this file was the level 1 file before and is now the level 2 file. For the level 3 file, select "Sage-Example-Diary-Level2.sav": select ID$ to be the L3id, no need for a level 2 id, and select CESDZ to be in the MDM. Note that this file was the level 2 file before and is now the level 3 file.

NB: HLM does not allow missing data at level 2 in a three-level MDM file. So, if you are using a level 1 file from a previous analysis (as we are doing here), you need to be certain that there are no missing values for the variables that you are including in the MDM file when you use this file at level 2. You can have missing values when a file is used as a level 1 file, but not when the same data are used as a level 2 file. Also, you have to include some type of variable (in addition to identifiers) at each level of analysis, even if you never intend to analyze that variable.

When setting up a three-level file such as this with the primary (or sole) purpose of estimating the item level reliability of a set of items, I sometimes enter some type of "nonsense" variable at levels 2 and 3 to keep the program happy. On the other hand, if you want to bring the level 1 intercept from such an analysis up to level 2, you should include predictors at levels 2 and 3, with the caveat that there can be no missing data at level 2.

Just as before, name the MDM file (I named it "rse-item.mdm"), and save the MDMT file (I named it "rse-item"; the .mdmt is automatically added). Click Make MDM. Click Check Stats. The HLM3MDM.STS file appears (note "3" replaces "2" compared to the name of the STS file for the example two-level model). There should be no surprises in this file. Assuming no missing observations, the number of level 1 observations should be a multiple of the number of level 2 observations (in our case, four). If the wrong number of observations appears, check the raw data files with special attention to how they were sorted. This file was renamed "rse-item.sts."

Finally, to run the analysis, select RSE as the outcome variable. To estimate the reliability of a scale, you need to run a totally unconditional model: so, no predictors at levels 2 or 3. Name the output (rse-item0.txt). Save the command file (rse-item.hlm). Run analysis. The model is presented as follows:

level 1 (item) $\quad y_{ijk} = \pi_{0jk} + e_{ijk}$

level 2 (day) $\quad \pi_{0jk} = \beta_{00k} + r_{0jk}$

level 3 (person) $\quad \beta_{00k} = \gamma_{000} + \mu_{00k}$

The critical part of the output is the reliability of the level 1 coefficient. Look for the text "Random level-1 coefficient Reliability estimate." The reliability for this measure is .505. This is the functional equivalent of a Cronbach's alpha for these four items considered as a scale, adjusted for both person level and day level variance. This is the Real McCoy – accept no substitutes.

Other parts of this analysis are worth noting, particularly in comparison to the results of the unconditional two-level model. The day level variance of self-esteem from the three-level model is .33567 (intercept variance, R0, under header "Final estimation of level-1 and level-2 variance components"). This is the variance of the average of the items, which is the same quantity as the day level (level 1) variance from the two-level model (rse0.txt). The day level variance estimate (R0) from the two-level analysis was .66477. The day level variance from the three-level model is lower than the day level variance from the two-level model because the three-level model takes into account the item level variability. In the two-level model, item level variability is not modeled and is included (more or less) in the day level variance. Another way to think about the difference is that the two-level model was analyzing observed means, whereas the three-level model was analyzing latent means.

Note, however, that the person level variance is virtually the same between the two models. For the three-level model this is the variance of the intercept of the intercepts (U00, .78898), and for the two-level model this is simply the variance of the intercept (U0, .79770). This similarity reflects the fact that the person level coefficients from the two models were equally reliable: the level 3 coefficient from the three-level model (B00, .936) and the intercept from the level 2 model (B0, .937). In other words, participants varied somewhat in terms of how they responded to the items across the days of the study, but there was considerable consistency in terms of how they responded overall (i.e., on average, across all items and all days).

Given all this, one might ask about the substantive implications of taking the item level variability into account. Does taking into account item level reliability change other coefficients that might be directly related to hypothesis testing, such as the within-person relationship between self-esteem and daily events? Such a possibility can be examined by conducting an analysis in which the level 1 intercept (mean response) is "brought up" to level 2 (now the item level) and modeled as function of daily events.

To conduct such an analysis, open the program with the three-level MDM file "loaded," click on Level 2, select POSMN, enter group-mean centered, toggle the error term (now at level 3). Name the output file (rse-item-posmn.txt). Save the command file (rse-item-posmn.hlm). Note that this three-level model is basically the two-level model from before, "piled on top" of the measurement model (now level 1). So, choices that were made at level 1 (e.g., entering daily predictors) are now made at level 2, and choices that were made at level 2 (e.g., toggling error terms) are now made at level 3.

Inspection of the output suggests that modeling the item level variability did not lead to meaningful changes in estimates of the types of effects that are typically the focus of hypotheses. More specifically, the estimates of parameters for the slope produced by this three-level model were not meaningfully different from the estimates provided by the two-level model (rse-posmn.txt). The mean slope was .553832 v. .554298, the t-ratio testing this slope was 7.804 v. 7.799, and the estimate of the random error term for the slope was .22716 v. .23354. Moreover, the relationships between CESD scores and intercepts and slopes produced by analyses of the two- and three-level models were very, very similar. I will spare you the details here, but you can compare the results yourself by running models in which CESDZ is included at level 3 as a predictor of slopes or intercepts from level 2. Just highlight a level 3 equation, select CESDZ, name the output file, save the command file, run the analysis, and examine the output (e.g., rse-item-cesdz.txt and rse-item.cesdz.hlm).

In data structures such as these (i.e., days within persons), I have not found important differences between the results of two-level models and three-level models with a measurement level added. As noted previously, it was the lack of such differences that led Shelly Gable and I to present the results of individual two-level models rather than the results of three-level models in Nezlek and Gable (2001). Nevertheless, this is the best way I know to estimate reliability within a multilevel data structure, and so these types of analyses serve a very important (perhaps limited) function. Moreover, it is possible that separating the item level variance from the variance of the next level of analysis might make an important difference under some circumstances. The only way to know this is to try it and get an idea about how the type of data you have react to such treatment.

Three-level analysis with a measurement level as the first level: analyzing multiple outcomes simultaneously

Although adding a measurement level to a model may not produce dramatic differences in some aspects of an analysis, it can provide some very important advantages over models that do not have a measurement level. One of these is the ability to analyze multiple outcomes simultaneously. Note that I do not describe such analyses as multivariate analyses. This is for two reasons. First, the term "multivariate analysis" has a specific referent within the HLM lexicon, something explained in a separate section later. Second, analyses of simultaneous outcomes in HLM do not produce the types of estimates of the relative contribution of an individual variable to a multivariate outcome that are provided in discriminant analysis. To me, the most important benefit of multiple outcome MLM is the ability to compare coefficients across different outcomes, and I illustrate this below.

In the study from which the test data were taken, a daily measure of Beck's triad was also collected (the TRI measure in the original level 1 data set). Just as the four self-esteem items could be modeled at the item level (latent level), the three items of the triad can be modeled, and these two sets of items can be modeled simultaneously. The critical feature of such analyses is that all items for all outcomes are nested simultaneously, and separate sets of coefficients are generated for each outcome by using dummy codes and a no-intercept model. This is similar to a technique introduced in Chapter 2 in the section "Categorical predictors and examining differences among groups."

The level 1 data file for this analysis is in the second panel of Table 7. Note that there are now seven responses (items) nested within each day. The self-esteem items have a sequence of 4 or less, and the triad measure has a sequence of 5, 6, or 7. Once again, the specific order of the items is not important, but the item file needs to be sorted in the same order as the other files in terms of the identifying fields (ID$, JDATE$). Note the addition of two variables, RSE and TRI, both dummy codes: RSE is set to 1 for self-esteem items and to 0 for triad items, and TRI is set to 1 for triad items and to 0 for self-esteem items.

The MDM file can be created by modifying the template file (the MDMT file) created when the MDM file was made for the item level analysis of self-esteem. Open the program, select "File," select "Make new MDM from old MDM template (.mdmt) file," select "rse-item.mdmt" (or whatever you named the template file for the item level analysis of self-esteem). First, the level 1 file needs to be changed. Under "Level-1 File Specification," click "Browse" and select "rse-tri-item.sav." Click "Choose Variables," select ID$ as the L3id, JDATE$ as the L2id, and add

RESP, RSE, and TRI to the MDM. Rename the MDM file (I renamed it "rse-tri-item. mdm"). Save the MDMT file. Make MDM.

Take a look at the STS file (of course). It was renamed "rse-tri-item.sts." Assuming all is well, set up the unconditional model. Select RESP as the outcome. Enter RSE and TRI uncentered. Make certain to toggle the error terms at level 2 and level 3 to include them. Drop the intercept: click on level 1 variable list, select intercept, select "Delete variable from model." Name output, "rse-tri-item0.txt." Save command file, "rse-tri-item0.hlm". Run analysis. The model is below. Note the lack of an intercept at level 1.

level 1 (item)	$y_{ijk} = \pi_{1jk}(\text{RSE}) + \pi_{2jk}(\text{TRI}) + e_{ijk}$
level 2 (day)	$\pi_{1jk} = \beta_{10k} + r_{1jk}$
	$\pi_{2jk} = \beta_{20k} + r_{2jk}$
level 3 (person)	$\beta_{10k} = \gamma_{100} + \mu_{10k}$
	$\beta_{20k} = \gamma_{200} + \mu_{20k}$

Comparing the parameter estimates for self-esteem from this analysis and from the three- and two-level models of self-esteem alone indicates that the person level variance and the estimate of the mean and the accompanying standard error are functionally equivalent across the three analyses. Of note is the fact that the item level reliability estimates of self-esteem produced by the two three-level models (RSE alone and RSE and TRI together) are different (.505 alone v. .634 together), and when self-esteem and the triad measure are analyzed together, the within-subject correlation is estimated. This correlation can be found under the heading "Tau(pi) (as correlations)," and it is .999. The between-subject correlation is .836, "Tau(beta) (as correlations)." Both the reliability estimates and the estimated correlations produced by such analyses need to be viewed with some caution, an issue I address below.

Nevertheless, the real power of modeling outcome simultaneously is the ability to compare slopes for different variables. Testing if the strength of the relationship between a level 1 predictor such as positive events and two different outcomes is different requires estimating a model in which both outcomes are included simultaneously. For a host of reasons (most notably the need to include the covariances among coefficients) it is not possible to run two analyses and compare the coefficients produced by such analyses.

For example, the following model could be used to compare the positive event slopes for RSE and TRI. This is done by constraining the γ_{110} and γ_{210} coefficients to be equal.

level 1 (item)	$y_{ijk} = \pi_{1jk}(\text{RSE}) + \pi_{2jk}(\text{TRI}) + e_{ijk}$
level 2 (day)	$\pi_{1jk} = \beta_{10k} + \beta_{11k}(\text{POSMN}) + r_{1jk}$
	$\pi_{2jk} = \beta_{20k} + \beta_{21k}(\text{POSMN}) + r_{2jk}$

level 3 (person) 　　$\beta_{10k} = \gamma_{100} + \mu_{10k}$

$\beta_{11k} = \gamma_{110} + \mu_{11k}$

$\beta_{20k} = \gamma_{200} + \mu_{20k}$

$\beta_{21k} = \gamma_{210} + \mu_{21k}$

The command file for this analysis is "rse-tri-item-posmn.hlm," and the output file is "rse-tri-item-posmn.txt." It is noteworthy that the model took over 1600 iterations to converge (using the default convergence criterion). Usually, this many iterations indicates that the program is having difficulty estimating a random error term. This was not the case in this instance because all the error terms were quite reliable: see last section of the output. Although it can be difficult to pinpoint the causes for a high number of iterations, in the present case, it is likely that the high correlation between RSE and TRI at the day level contributed to this.

　　Regardless, the analysis found that the slope between self-esteem and positive events (.556) was significantly different from the slope between the triad measure and positive events (.824). See the section of the output "Results of General Linear Hypothesis Testing," $\chi^2(1) = 21.5997$, $p < .001$. Moreover, predictors can be added at level 3 (the person) that would permit tests of differences in the strength of moderating relationships. For example, CESDZ scores could be added to the equations for the two slopes (β_{11k} and β_{21k}) and the resulting coefficients (γ_{111} and γ_{211}) could be constrained to be equal. I will allow you the privilege of doing this one on your own.

level 1 (item)　　　$y_{ijk} = \pi_{1jk} (RSE) + \pi_{2jk} (TRI) + e_{ijk}$

level 2 (day)　　　$\pi_{1jk} = \beta_{10k} + \beta_{11k} (POSMN) + r_{1jk}$

$\pi_{2jk} = \beta_{20k} + \beta_{21k} (POSMN) + r_{2jk}$

level 3 (Person)　　$\beta_{10k} = \gamma_{100} + \gamma_{101} (CESDZ) + \mu_{10k}$

$\beta_{11k} = \gamma_{110} + \gamma_{111} (CESDZ) + \mu_{11k}$

$\beta_{20k} = \gamma_{200} + \gamma_{201} (CESDZ) + \mu_{20k}$

$\beta_{21k} = \gamma_{210} + \gamma_{211} (CESDZ) + \mu_{21k}$

Analyzing multiple outcomes simultaneously: some caveats

For most users, I offer three caveats about such analyses of multiple outcomes. First, I do not recommend (quite strongly) using the reliability estimates from such analyses to understand the item level reliability (akin to Cronbach's alpha) of a set of items. All estimates in a MLM are contingent upon the exact model specified (e.g., the predictors in the model, error structure, etc.). They are not the result of a process in which the calculations for an outcome are done in isolation from the calculations for another outcome. Note that the item level reliability for self-esteem varied across the two analyses (i.e., RSE only v. RSE and TRI together). When the items for a scale are analyzed in isolation without any predictors at any level of analysis, this produces as "pure" an estimate of the item level reliability as you can get. When any predictors are entered (or when another outcome is modeled simultaneously), this produces an estimate of what is called "conditional" reliability – an estimate of the reliability that is conditional, i.e., an estimate based on the specific conditions of a model.

Not quite as strongly, but with vigor, I recommend caution when interpreting the estimates of correlations between measures provided by analyses of multiple outcomes. Once again, it is important to keep in mind that these correlations are estimates, based on covariances, which themselves are conditional on the model being conducted. The correlations estimated by a MLM are not correlations that are produced by some formula that is some type of variation on the calculation of a Pearson's r. Including another variable (e.g., adding a third variable to two) changes the estimated correlation between the original variables. How much this changes cannot be predicted (or at least I have not been able to predict it).

Finally, and more practically, keep in mind that when you set up a data file for use this way, you have to analyze the data using all the outcomes specified by the level 1 (item level) model. If you have the items for two outcomes, you have to analyze both of them. If you have items for three outcomes, you have to analyze all three. This means that if you decide to drop an outcome from an analysis, you need to recreate the level 1 file and then recreate the MDM file.

Robust parameter estimates

For tests of fixed effects, HLM provides two sets of parameter estimates – robust and non-robust. Robust estimates are more desirable because they provide a better basis for making inferences about the population; they are more "robust" in terms of overcoming the vagaries of sampling. Note that the non-robust estimates are not labeled as such, whereas the robust estimates are. Both are at the end of the output (non-robust followed by robust). One nice thing about robust versus non-robust parameter estimates is that the decision rule is simple. Use the robust estimates unless the program tells you not to use them. The decision to use robust estimates is based upon the number of level 2 units, with 30 being a sort of minimum for the use of robust estimates, at least in my experience.

Some concluding thoughts

There are a few topics that I chose not to discuss in this volume. These were primarily advanced topics that are probably not that relevant to many or most social and personality psychologists, and there were the limitations of space. Nevertheless, I will discuss them briefly here in the interest of describing some of the important options that exist in HLM.

I have not explicitly discussed analyses of data collected within couples. To nest individuals within couples is certainly appropriate. Nevertheless, there are a variety of ways in which coupled data can be analyzed (both within and outside of the multilevel context), and I recommend consulting Kenny, Kashy, and Cook (2006) for a thorough discussion of analyzing data collected for couples.

There is also the matter of the HMLM and HMLM2 MDM files. The first M stands for "multivariate." Although the title suggests that such data structures would be relevant for some or even many social and personality psychology applications, this is not really the case. In these data structures, there is a measurement level that is similar in some ways to the measurement level used in analyses of simultaneous outcomes (described earlier). The critical and essential difference is that the measurement occasions are fixed rather than random, such as in a longitudinal study in which observations are collected every year, every six months, and so forth.

Although such multivariate models provide more flexibility to model error structures for the level 1 observations than is provided in the standard HLM structure (e.g., autocorrelation), aside from longitudinal studies in which there are multiple observations that occur at fixed intervals, these multivariate analyses are not really a good match for most/many of the data structures collected by social and personality psychologists. For example, as discussed a while back, in a daily diary study, the days over which the study is conducted are not fixed. They are randomly sampled. In contrast, in a longitudinal study of children at ages 1, 3, 5, and 7, the measurement occasions (ages) are not random effects. They are fixed effects. In a study in which people are nested within groups, none of the alternatives offered by the multivariate option can be applied.

Finally, because I am certain some of you are curious, HLM cannot do multilevel factor analysis. My sense is that the best program for doing multilevel factor analysis is Mplus; there may be others. It is my belief however that the present understanding of multilevel factor analysis is somewhat limited. That is, present algorithms provide the basis for estimating an overall solution, but do not provide a basis for estimating solutions for level 2 (or higher) units of analysis. So, in a diary study, it is possible to estimate the overall within-person factor structure, corrected for all sorts of differences between people, but it is not possible to estimate factor structures for individuals and then model the differences among them. Half a loaf is better than none, however, and it is possible that techniques that can model individual differences in factor structures may appear in the future.

I wrote this volume as a sort of summary of what I teach in the workshops I give, and many of the issues that I discuss here have been raised by the participants in these workshops. I hope you have found the discussion helpful. Please keep in mind, however, that this volume is simply an introduction, a description of basic techniques and principles. It is now your responsibility to take these tools and use them to answer the questions that matter to you. *Bon voyage*!

References

Affleck, G., Zautra, A., Tennen, H., & Armeli, S. (1999). Multilevel daily process designs for consulting and clinical psychology: A preface for the perplexed. *Journal of Consulting and Clinical Psychology, 67*, 746–754.

Aiken, L. S., & West, S. G. (1991). *Multiple regression: Testing and interpreting interactions.* Newbury Park, CA: Sage.

Baron, R. A., & Kenny, D. M. (1986). The moderator–mediator variable distinction in social psychological research: Conceptual, strategic, and statistical considerations. *Journal of Personality and Social Psychology, 51*, 1173–1182.

Bauer, D. J., Preacher, K. J., & Gil, K. M. (2006). Conceptualizing and testing random indirect effects and moderated mediation in multilevel models: New procedures and recommendations. *Psychological Methods, 11*, 142–163.

Bryk, A. S., & Raudenbush, S. W. (1992). *Hierarchical linear models.* Newbury Park, CA: Sage.

Cervone, D. (2004). Personality architecture: Within-person structures and processes. *Annual Reviews, 56*, 423–452.

Cohen, J., & Cohen, P. (1983). *Applied multiple regression correlation analysis for the behavioral sciences.* Hillsdale, NJ: Erlbaum.

Enders, C. K., & Tofighi, D. (2007). Centering predictor variables in cross-sectional multilevel models: A new look at an old issue. *Psychological Methods, 12*, 121–138.

Kenny, D. A., Kashy, D. A., & Cook, W. L. (2006). *Dyadic data analysis.* New York: Guilford.

Kleinbaum, D. G., & Klein, M. (2002). *Logistic regression: A self-learning text* (2nd ed.). New York: Springer.

Kreft, I. G. G., & de Leeuw, J. (1998). *Introducing multilevel modeling.* Newbury Park, CA: Sage.

Littell, R. C., Milliken, G. A., Stroup, W. W., & Wolfinger, R. D. (1996). *SAS system for mixed models.* Cary, NC: SAS Institute.

Maas, C. J. M., & Hox, J. J. (2005). Sufficient sample sizes for multilevel modeling. *Methodology, 1*, 86–92.

Marsh, H. W., & Hau, K. (2003). Big-fish-little-pond effect on academic self-concept: A cross-cultural (26 country) test of the negative effects of academically selective schools. *American Psychologist, 58*, 364–376.

Matsumoto, D., Nezlek, J. B., & Koopman, B. (2007). Evidence for universality in phenomenological emotion response system coherence. *Emotion, 7*, 57–67.

Nezlek, J. B. (2001). Multilevel random coefficient analyses of event and interval contingent data in social and personality psychology research. *Personality and Social Psychology Bulletin, 27,* 771–785.

Nezlek, J. B. (2002). Day-to-day relationships between self-awareness, daily events, and anxiety. *Journal of Personality, 70,* 249–275.

Nezlek, J. B. (2005). Distinguishing affective and non-affective reactions to daily events. *Journal of Personality, 73,* 1539–1568.

Nezlek, J. B., & Gable, S. L. (2001). Depression as a moderator of relationships between positive daily events and day-to-day psychological adjustment. *Personality and Social Psychology Bulletin, 27,* 1692–1704.

Nezlek, J. B., Kafetsios, K., & Smith, C. V. (2008). Emotions in everyday social encounters: Correspondence between culture and self-construal. *Journal of Cross-Cultural Psychology, 39,* 366–372. DOI 10.1177/0022022108318114.

Nezlek, J. B., & Kuppens, P. (2008). Regulating positive and negative emotions in daily life. *Journal of Personality, 76,* 561–580.

Nezlek, J. B., & Plesko, R. M. (2003). Affect- and self-based models of relationships between daily events and daily well-being. *Personality and Social Psychology Bulletin, 29,* 584–596.

Nezlek, J. B., & Smith, C. V. (2005). Social identity in daily social interaction. *Self and Identity, 4,* 243–261.

Nezlek, J. B., Sorrentino, R. M., Yasunaga, S., Otsubo, Y., Allen, M., Kouhara, S., & Shuper, P. (2008). Cross-cultural differences in reactions to daily events as indicators of cross-cultural differences in self-construction and affect. *Journal of Cross-Cultural Psychology, 39,* 685–702. DOI 10.1177/0022022108323785.

Rabash, J., Steele, F., Browne, W. J., & Goldstein, H. (2009). *A user's guide to MLwiN, v2.10.* Centre for Multilevel Modelling, University of Bristol.

Radloff, L. S. (1977). The CES–D scale: A self report depression scale for research in the general population. *Applied Psychological Measurement, 1,* 385–401.

Raudenbush, S. W., & Bryk, A. S. (2002). *Hierarchical linear models* (2nd ed.). Newbury Park, CA: Sage.

Richter, T. (2006). What is wrong with ANOVA and multiple regression? Analyzing sentence reading times with hierarchical linear models. *Discourse Analysis, 41,* 221–250.

Robinson, W. S. (1950). Ecological correlations and the behavior of individuals. *American Sociological Review, 15,* 351–357.

Rosenberg, M. (1965). *Society and the adolescent self-image.* Princeton, NJ: Princeton University Press.

Scherbaum, C. M., & Ferreter, J. M. (2009). Estimating statistical power and required sample sizes for organizational research using multilevel modeling. *Organizational Research Methods, 12,* 237–367.

Tomprou, M., Nikoloau, I., & Nezlek, J. B. (2010). Psychological Contract Creation upon Newcomer's Organisational Entry: Honeymoon period or Reality Shock? Unpublished manuscript: Athens University of Economics & Business.

Resources

Aiken, L. S., & West, S. G. (1991). *Multiple regression: Testing and interpreting interactions*. Newbury Park, CA: Sage.
A classic. This books explains pretty much all you need to know about interactions within the multiple regression. You probably own a copy already. If not, get one.

Kreft, I. G. G., & de Leeuw, J. (1998). *Introducing multilevel modeling*. Newbury Park, CA: Sage.
An excellent introduction to MLM with a very informative Q&A format.

Littell, R. C., Milliken, G. A., Stroup, W. W., & Wolfinger, R. D. (1996). *SAS System for mixed models*. Cary, NC: SAS Institute.
All you ever wanted to know about random coefficient modeling and more. A definite must for SAS-aholics.

Rabash, J., Steele, F., Browne, W. J., & Goldstein, H. (2009). *A user's guide to MLwiN, v2.10*. Centre for Multilevel Modelling, University of Bristol.
Similar to the user's guide for HLM, this manual is itself a text about multilevel modeling. The style is a bit formal, lots of equations (not in the Raudenbush & Bryk style), and the nomenclature is geared to the program itself, but the coverage of various topics is excellent. Can be downloaded for free.

Raudenbush, S. W., & Bryk, A. S. (2002). *Hierarchical linear models* (2nd ed.). Newbury Park, CA: Sage.
One of the classic references in the field. It was written with the HLM software in mind, so readers can read the book, run some analyses, and compare what they have done with what they read. I did this for a few years and still do from time to time.

Singer, J. D. (1998). Using SAS PROC MIXED to fit multilevel models, hierarchical models, and individual growth models. *Journal of Educational and Behavioral Statistics*, *23*, 323–355.
A good introduction about how to use SAS to conduct MLM.

Snijders, T., & Bosker, R. (1999). *Multilevel analysis*. London: Sage.
A solid introduction to MLM by two experienced modelers.

Index

aggregation 7, 10
analysis of aggregates 5
ANOVA 45, 73
asymmetries, HLM 86
autocorrelated errors 4

backward stepping 32
Baron, R. A. 41
Bauer, D. J. 41–4
Bayes estimators 45
Bayes residuals 22–4
Bayes shrinkage 45–6, 48
Beck's triad 39, 75, 100
between-class level 12–13
between-group level 4, 5–7
between-level interactions 36–41, 86–9
between-person analysis 6
between-person difference 41
between-person level 9
between-person variance 47
Big Fish in a Little Pond Effect
    (BFLPE) 18–19
binomial distribution 50
binomial outcome 51
Bryk, A. S. 9, 10, 17, 18, 72
buffering effect 40

carrying capacity 33, 56
categorical predictors 26–9
categorical responses 50–1
categorical variables, centering 17
causality, modeling 48–50
centering 13–19
    changing centering, 83
    see also grand-mean centering; group-mean
        centering
    HLM 83
    reporting guidelines 66
chi-squared test 25, 93
classical test theory 44

coefficient comparison 25–6, 60, 61, 92–3
    different signs 94–5
    simultaneous outcomes 100
command files, HLM 80–2, 95, 102
confounding variance 57–8
contextual effects, multi-level random
        coefficient models 18–19
continuous outcomes 10–11, 50
continuous variables, centering 17, 37, 38
contrast codes 26–9
convergence criterion 34, 80
correlation 5–6, 9–10, 14
    intra-class 53–4, 79
    multiple outcomes 103
    reliability 10
covariance 20, 21, 48
    diagnostics 34
    intra-class correlation 54
    matrices 30–1, 34
Cronbach's alpha 46–7
cross-classification 59, 76
cross-level interactions (between-level
        interactions) 36–41, 86–9
cross-level relationship, causality 49–50

data management 59–60, 103
data preparation 33, 72–5
data sorting 73–5
data stacking 42
data structure 66
de Leeuw, J. 1
dependent variables, categorical 26
descriptive statistics 29–30, 67, 71
deviance statistics 32, 33, 35
diagnostics 33–4
diary study 3, 4–5, 8, 9–10, 104
    centering 17
    data preparation 72–5
    HLM example 78–103
    interactions 36, 37, 38

diary study *cont.*
  missing data 61–2
  multilevel structure 53, 54–5, 56–8
  nesting 13
  non-linear outcomes 51
  reliability 46–7
  standardization 61
  variance 30
disaggregation techniques 7, 8
dummy codes 17, 26–9, 33–4, 42, 44, 49–50, 51
  intra-class correlation 54
  LSDV 8
  multilevel structure 57
  simultaneous outcomes 100
dummy variables 51, 63

ecological fallacy 7
effect size
  HLM 82–3, 85–6
  residual variance 35, 36
error 3–4
  see also random error
  autocorrelated 4
  HLM 88–9, 104
  LSDV 8
  model fit 32–3
  modeling 19–25, 34, 67
  multilevel random coefficient models 12, 19–25
  OLS 20
  type I 26
error variance, reliability 45
estimated Bayes (EB) coefficients 23, 24
estimated Bayes (EB) residuals 22–4
estimation algorithm, local minima 34

factor analysis, multi-level 104
fixed coefficients 12, 22, 24
fixed components 33
fixed effects 21–2, 27, 29, 33
  HLM 85, 88, 92
  model building 30–1
  non-linear outcomes 50
  residual variance 36
  t-ratios 68
fixed predictors, HLM 84
fixed terms 32–3
fixed variance 20–1
flat file 38–9, 71, 86
forward stepping 32

Gable, S. 99
gamma coefficients 67–8

general linear hypothesis testing 93, 102
Gil, K. M. 41–4
grand-mean centering 14, 15–17, 18–19, 27, 40, 82
  HLM 83, 85, 86, 90–1
  standardization 61
graphs, presentations 68
group-mean centering 15, 16, 17–19
  continuous measures 38
  HLM 85, 86, 90–1, 99
  indicator variables 44

Hau, K. 18
HLM program 22, 33–4, 69–70, 71–104
  cross-classification 59
  cross-level interactions 37
  data management 60
  error covariance 34
  free version 70, 74
  missing data 62, 72–3, 76–7, 78, 91–2, 97
  nomenclature 13
  non-linear analysis 52
  reliability 46
HMLM files 104
HMLM2 files 104

"id" variables 74, 97, 100
independence of observations 8
independent variables, categorical 26
indicator variables 42–4
interaction 36–41
  HLM 89
  terms 37–8, 39
intercept 11, 12
  Bayes residuals 23–4
  categorical predictors 27, 28
  centering 13–14, 16, 18–19
  dummy codes 33–4
  HLM 81, 85, 87–8, 90, 92–3, 98–9, 101
  reliability 45, 46–7
intra-class correlation (ICC) 53–4, 79
iterations, convergence 34

Kafetsios, K. 30
Kenny, D. M. 41
Koopman, B. 30
Kreft, I. G. G. 1
Kuppens, P. 22

lagged relationships 49
lagged variables 74
least-squared dummy variable analysis (LSDV) 8, 54

linear dependence 33
link function 52
local minima 34
logistical regression 50–1
longitudinal studies 104

Marsh, H. W. 18
Matsumoto, D. 30
maximum likelihood estimates 21, 33, 36
MDM files 33, 59, 71, 72, 74–5, 84, 104
    creation 75–9
    example data 77–9
    simultaneous outcomes 103
    three-level analysis 97, 98, 100–1
MDMT files 71–2, 76, 78–9, 80, 91–2, 98, 101
mean
    group differences 27, 28–9
    OLS 14
    reliability 10, 45, 46
mean centering 37–8
measurement model 46
measurement theory 44
mediation 41–4
missing data 61–3
    HLM 62, 72–3, 76–7, 78, 91–2, 97
missing observations 61–2
misspecified models 21
MLwiN 34, 59, 69–70
model building 29–33, 87
model constraint, 25–6, 92, 94
model equations 66–7
model fit 31–2, 33
    deviance statistics 35
    HLM 92–3
    local minima 34
    reporting 68
modeling error 19–25, 34, 67
moderated mediation 41–2
moderated relationships 37, 93–4
    see also cross-level interactions
moderation 41–4
Monte Carlo studies 46
Mplus 104
multilevel factor analysis 104
multilevel random coefficient models 7
    advanced topics 35–52
    basics 9–34
multiple membership 58–9
multiple outcomes, simultaneous analysis 100–3
multivariate analysis 100, 104

Nezlek, J. B. 22, 30, 39, 42, 49, 62, 99
Nikolaou, I. 42

no-intercept model 28, 100
non-linear outcomes 11, 50–2
non-randomly varying coefficients 22
non-randomly varying models 21, 22
non-robust parameter estimation 103
null model *see* unconditional model

odds ratio 51
ordinary least squares (OLS) regression
    2, 7, 64, 65
    centering 13–14
    error terms 20
    independence of observations 8
    interactions 37, 38
    reliability 45
    residual variance 35, 36
    stepping 32–3
outliers 48
output files, HLM 79–82, 84–5, 102

parameter estimation
    carrying capacity 33
    centering 16
    HLM 101
    random error 21
    robust and non-robust 103
"passing up" 9
person-level relationships 30, 60
person-level variance 98–9, 101
Plesko, R. M. 39
population-average estimates 52
power, sample size 64–5
Preacher, K. J. 41–4
predicted values
    generation 38–40
    illustrating results 68
predictors
    see also centering
    categorical 26–9
    causality 48
    fixed 84
    HLM 82–9
    linear dependence 33
    multilevel random coefficient models 12–13
publication, reporting guidelines 65–8

random coefficients 12
random components 33
random effects, model building 30–1
random error 12, 20, 21–2, 24
    diagnostics 34
    HLM 84, 85, 88, 99
    model building 30–2

random error *cont.*
  modeling 67
  residual variance 35
randomly varying models 21, 22
random sampling 20
random terms 32–3, 36
random variance 20, 45
Raudenbush, S. W. 9, 10, 17, 18, 72
regression by groups analysis 64
reliability 44–8
  convergence problems 34
  correlation 10
  HLM 81, 95–100, 101, 102–3
  simultaneous outcomes 102–3
  three-level analysis 95–100,
    101, 102
repeated measures *see* diary studies
repeated measures ANOVA 73
reporting guidelines 65–8
residual error *see* random error
residual variances 35–6
reverse scores 47
Robinson, W. S. 7
robust parameter estimation 103
RSP files 71

sample size
  power 64–5
  reliability 10
sampling 20
sampling error 3–4
SAS 69
sequential models 68
significance *see* statistical significance
simultaneous outcomes 100–3
"slopes as outcomes" analysis 13, 17, 37
  see also cross-level interactions
  HLM 86–9
Smith, C. V. 30, 62
software 69–70
  see also HLM; MLwiN
  Mplus 104
  SPSS 74, 75, 77
sorting variables 73–5
SPSS 74, 75, 77
SSM files 71
stacking data 42
standard deviation
  HLM 86, 88
  standardization 61
  STS files 71
  within-level 38–9
standardization 18–19, 26, 60–1, 82, 83

statistical significance 12
  model building 30, 31
  random error 21, 24, 31
  residual variance 36
  variance 46
stepping 32–3
string variables 74
STS files 71, 72, 76, 77, 78–9,
  86, 101

test scores 12–13, 14
three-level models 10–11
  HLM 76
  interactions 36–7, 38
  measurement level as first level 100–2
  missing data 62
  multilevel structure 56–7
  reliability estimation 95–100
tight models 33
time, causality 49–50
Tomprou, M. 42
totally unconditional model 11
total variance 44, 81
transformation 60
  HLM 74–5
  non-linear outcomes 50, 52
t-ratios 68, 82, 83, 99
triad measure 39
true variance 44–5, 81
two-level models 4
  Bayes shrinkage 45
  continuous outcomes 10–11
  data management 59–60
  HLM 76
  interactions 36–8
  level of entry 55
  missing data 62
  modeling error 22–4
  standardization 60–1
type I error 26

uncentering *see* zero centering
unconditional models 11, 12, 16, 29–30
  HLM 79–82, 83–4, 85, 90, 101
  SD 39
  standardization 61
unit-specific estimates 52

variance
  between-person 47
  centering 16
  confounding 57–8
  fixed coefficients 24

variance *cont.*
  HLM 81–3, 85–6, 88, 90, 98–9, 100
  intra-class correlation 53–4
  modeling error 20–1
  multi-level random coefficient models
    11, 20–1
  non-linear outcomes 50
  person level 98–9, 101
  random 20, 45
  reduction 35, 86
  reliability 10, 44–6, 81
  residual 35–6
  standardization 61
  STS files 71
  total 44, 81
  true 44–5, 81
  unconditional models 29–30
  within-group 10, 11
  within-level interaction 38–9
  within-person 47

weighted indicator variables 59
within-class level 12, 19
within couples analysis 104
within-group level 4, 5–7
within-group variance 10
  multi-level random coefficient models 11
within-level interactions 36–41
  moderation 41
within-level standard deviation 38–9
within-person analysis 6–7, 56
  HLM 85–6
within-person level 9
within-person relationships 3
within-person variance 47
within-unit standard deviation 71

zero centering 14–17, 61, 83, 84, 85
zero-order relationship 42
zero-point 17
z-scores 82, 83